Copyright © 2002 James Armstrong
All rights reserved.

ISBN 1-58898-710-8

Feet of Clay on Solid Ground

James Armstrong

greatunpublished.com
Title No. 710
2002

Feet of Clay on Solid Ground

CONTENTS

Introduction		ix
Chapter I	"You Should Have Been a Priest"	1
Chapter II	"If I Had a Thousand Lives to Live"	9
Chapter III	"You Ain't Fit to Be No Methodist Preacher"	35
Chapter IV	"A Leader Must Be a Bridge"	53
Chapter V	"I Am Absolutely Responsible"	71
Chapter VI	"The Call Has Not Been Canceled"	85
Chapter VII	"New Alphas"	101
Epilogue as Prologue		119
June of 2000		125
Notes		127

INTRODUCTION

In one of his most oft-quoted phrases F. Scott Fitzgerald said, "There are no second acts in American life."(1) He was wrong.

In May of 1982, the *U.S. News and World Report* called me "the most influential religious leader in the United States." The *Christian Century* listed me among "the most influential." Without question the recognition came as a result of my election to the presidency of the National Council of Churches, but it was pretty heady stuff. I was riding the crest of a wave of public recognition, and, undeserved as it may have been, it was profoundly satisfying. Then my world collapsed.

On November 16, 1983, I resigned as President of the National Council and as a bishop of the United Methodist Church. Entrusting my letter of resignation to the hands of a trusted friend I sent it to the Council of Bishops meeting in San Francisco. The opening words of my statement were: "I am absolutely responsible for all that follows. I have been unfaithful to my wife and family." Nothing could have been more clear. However, my colleagues meeting in San Francisco, after consulting with NCC officials and members of my family, refashioned the statement. They changed it to read: "I have submitted myself to an exhausting and inhuman work schedule and because of this have failed many persons as well as the Gospel."

After dispatching my letter I climbed into my car and headed westward toward Denver. From time to time I would stop by the wayside and call San Francisco. Somewhere in central Illinois I was told of the revision of my resignation statement.

Wanting to be truthful, wanting to put the shock elements of the statement behind me, I argued for the original wording only to be told that the bishops of the church, ecumenical leaders in New York, and my family wanted the altered version. Reluctantly, after several more futile phone calls, I agreed for the sake (I thought) of everyone involved. The statement, in terms of intentions and consequence the same as the original, was far different in essence. Immediately the conjecture began. Had Armstrong had a "nervous breakdown?" Had he "burned out?" Was he an alcoholic, a homosexual, a womanizer, a drug addict? The speculation had begun. That was almost twenty years ago.

In 1984, Bishop John A.T. Robinson died. Commenting on his death the press referred to him as a defense witness in the obscenity trial of *Lady Chatterly's Lover*, as a notable who had praised *Playboy* nudity, as a leading churchman who had questioned the Virgin Birth and the Second Coming of Christ. Author of *Honest to God* he was called a "heretic" and somehow was held responsible for "the death of God" movement. There is no question that, influenced by Dietrich Bonhoeffer, Paul Tillich and Rudolf Bultman, he had offered a fresh and invigorating version of classic Christianity. Like today's Episcopal Bishop John Shelby Spong he had insisted that true Christian faith is not a collection of stale beliefs and static moralisms. Robinson was a daring adventurer who never disavowed the basics of faith, *but how would he be remembered?* Would those who had reduced him to a handful of sensational negatives have the last word? I could not help but see a parallel. How would I be remembered – if at all?

Reuben Askew, a former governor of Florida, was a Democratic hopeful during a presidential primary in the mid-'80s. His campaign never got off the ground. He suffered from a lack of name and face recognition beyond his home state. Even in Florida, where he had been an effective and popular leader, he was no longer in the public eye. After his failed efforts in 1984, he returned to his law practice and normal routine. One day in Miami an elderly woman squinted at him quizzically, approached him and asked, "Didn't you used to be Reuben Askew?"(2) Of course he had been and continued to be. Nor did Jim Armstrong become past tense with his resignation from positions of church leadership. Life has continued, with many twists and turns, to become an ever more satisfying and adventuresome journey. The first act did come to an end. Other acts, however, would follow.

This slender volume began to take shape following my resignation. A first draft was completed within a year. Thank God that version was never published. Time has passed, I have distanced myself from the events of November '83, lessons have been learned and applied, and I have crisscrossed the country from Indianapolis to Florida to the District of Columbia to Denver and back to Florida again. I believe it is a story worth telling.

*Dedicated to the memory of
R. Benjamin Garrison, a lifelong friend and colleague.*

CHAPTER I

"YOU SHOULD HAVE BEEN A PRIEST"

Our oldest son had just graduated from high school. We were sitting in the living room of our home in Indianapolis talking about the days ahead, forthcoming activities related to the end of the school year, my complicated schedule and how, once again, my commitments would foul up our plans as a family. Jim said, "Dad, you should have been a priest." It wasn't said in anger or as an accusation. He wasn't trying to be funny. Just a matter-of-fact comment: "Dad, you should have been a priest."

I'm no fan of celibacy but there was more than a germ of truth in what he said. As a father I was not as available as our youngsters deserved and needed me to be. As a husband I was not as thoughtful and attentive as I should have been. My speaking engagements, early morning study habits, outside commitments, civic involvements and willingness to respond to every Tom, Dick and Mary coming down the pike negated the possibility of a stable, balanced, healthy home life.

I can't blame my parents. In retrospect they seemed to provide an almost perfect balance. Mother was a prim and proper woman, gentle, intelligent, sensitive, deeply religious, easily shocked at the turn of a crude phrase. She had been a schoolteacher and was an "ideal preacher's wife" as people used to say.

But Dad was no stereotypical preacher. Growing up in the rough 'n tumble of western Montana, he had his nose broken three times – football, baseball and boxing (he was a lightweight contender as an amateur). He enlisted in the National Guard and was sent off to the Mexican border in 1916 when Pancho Villa's band of revolutionaries crossed into New Mexico. His best friend, our legendary "Uncle Andy," was a Kalispell saloonkeeper's son who was killed in the trenches of France just hours before the armistice was signed in 1918. Irene, Andy's sister, was an early, fairly serious fling. No stranger to carousing Dad's was a "hell-raising" youth. He would love to have been a doctor but funds and opportunity did not seem available in the remote regions of the northwest frontier, so he followed in his father's footsteps and became a preacher.

He was no longer a lightweight when I entered his world. He was a lovable bear of a man who was equally at home wearing an apron in the kitchen, helping farmers with their plowing, tucking a toothpick in the back of his mouth as he kissed his little boy good night, or brawling with a hardware merchant who called him a "sonofabitch." He was tempestuous, warm hearted, good natured, a rebellious sort of maverick who was never far beyond the reach of his loved ones.

I was a seminary student in Atlanta when my father died. A brain hemorrhage claimed him when he was only 58. I can't describe my sense of loss. Although separated by the width of a continent for a few years we had remained extremely close. Driving across the southwestern desert in my battered old car, bound for Victorville and his funeral, I heard the melody, "Going Home" on my car radio and found myself unashamedly sobbing.

When I was elected to the United Methodist episcopacy in 1968, Mother was as proud as any mother could be. Dad would have been proud too – with all sorts of reservations. He would have shaken his head, guffawed, and said, "My gawd, Jim, what have they done to you?" Mother died in 1976. I'm glad neither one of them had to suffer through my resignation in 1983.

I was 15 when Phyllis Jeanne, attractive and vivacious daughter of Mildred and Glenn Shaeffer, became a part of my life. She lived next door to Johnny Elder, my best friend. I had a mountain climbing accident, had fallen nearly 50 feet and had fractured my skull and shattered both legs (a doctor said I wouldn't be walking within 15 years). I was laid up with casts up to my hips, enduring a slow and deadly boring recovery, when Johnny suggested that Phyllis bring me a stack of his comic books. That's how it all began.

For the next two years Phyllis and I were inseparable. I carried her books between classes at school. There was church; there were movies and proms and the corner drug store. There was groping in parked cars and the excitement of adolescent discovery. Barely out of high school we discovered she was pregnant. We were married on July 26, 1942. We were both 17.

Everyone from Dr. Spock to Dr. Laura would agree that the union was ill-fated from the start. We were far too young; we came from radically different backgrounds; our worlds of experience were terribly limited. But, the year was 1942, and in those days there was only one "honorable" thing to do. Anyway, we thought we were in love. We moved 2500 miles across the country, from southern California to Florida, in order to prove we could make it on our own.

Our firstborn was a strapping boy we named Jimmie (Arthur James III). His skull had not grown together properly and the prognosis was not good. I had the night shift and night after night, clutching curly-headed little "Jimbo" in my arms, I paced back and forth across our living room, humming tuneless songs and praying to whatever might be out there. Jim survived, grew into a devilishly handsome, charming, fun-filled young man. A natural born salesman, but also a free spirit, he turned from sales to become a brilliant artist, immersed in Hopi legends and themes of the great Southwest. Today his works are displayed across the country.

Fifteen months after Jim's birth Terri was born. Across the years she has endured more than her share of heartache and sadness, but has done so with unbelievable grit and determination. She is bright beyond belief, has been a fabulous single mother (and grandmother), and in spite of everything, has maintained a raucous, contagious sense of humor. An unreconstructed idealist she is Program Director for Healthy Families, an organization that deals with child abuse and dysfunctional families.

Then came John. In April 1946, I was serving a small Methodist "student appointment" on the west coast of Florida while attending Florida Southern College. Our town had no hospital. Its mayor, a naturopath, was the closest thing we had to a "real" doctor. When Phyllis' labor pains began we made a mad scramble for the nearest hospital twenty miles away. Our friend the mayor was nowhere to be found, so a hardy nurse and I delivered little John. Unforgettable! Today John is a "gentleman farmer" in South Georgia where he and his wife, Susan, raise Pasofino show horses. He serves as Lay Leader and Sunday School superintendent in his little country church.

Becky was born in 1950. A beautiful child she was "Queen" of her kindergarten class. She has been an omnicompetent fixture in our nation's capitol for the past 25 years, first serving on Senator George McGovern's staff, then becoming Senator Bennett Johnston's "girl Friday." She was his personal secretary until his retirement in 1997, when she became the Office Manager of his D.C. consulting firm.

Becky and Ed Putens were married in October, 1975, in a private ceremony in the McGovern home. Ed is Roman Catholic so Father Robert Drinan, a good friend and former congressman (when first elected to Congress his youthful supporters strung a banner across his Boston headquarters that read, "Our Father, who art in Congress") officiated with me.

Seven years after Becky's birth little Leslye Grace put in her appearance. Her childhood nickname, "Pooh" (after "Winnie the...") captured something of her pixish manner. Her high school years were spent in Aberdeen, South Dakota. During those years her mother was living much of the time in Florida as an interior designer and I did a lot of the parenting, forging a very special bond with our youngest.

Many years ago Leslye was diagnosed with Multiple Sclerosis. Married to David Hope and the mother of three, she has handled her illness with rare grace and strength. In remission now, she exudes a loving, devil-may-care disposition that is a gift to all of us. True to her name, she gives us *hope*.

The foregoing recital may seem like one of those Christmas letters detailing all sorts of family information that no one outside a very limited circle really cares about, but there is a moral to my story. In my 1983 resignation statement I confessed that I had failed my family and loved ones—and I had.

In Chapter V, I will describe the traumatic confrontations with our kids following the resignation. The disbelief, the hurt and sense of betrayal ran deep. But, through the years that followed amends have been made, we more fully understand one another, have become available to one another, and today share a valued closeness. Each of the youngsters, now moving through the middle years of life, is a unique creation, each survived to become a remarkably fine human being in spite of a less-than-perfect childhood. Since personal failure and family considerations stood at the center of my demise from leadership in the church I felt I should write about these matters openly before moving on to describe education and career.

Now, let me go back. During our earliest years Phyllis was a slave to circumstance. Five children had entered her life, the first four clustered together in short order. While still a teenager she found herself changing diapers (well before Pampers were in vogue), washing, ironing, cooking, cleaning and all the rest. She made most of the girls' clothes and kept the boys patched together. Later she would say that she seemed to be in a haze much of that time, hardly conscious of her coming and going, functioning on the basis of sheer necessity.

Later, although she would have "help" with the housework, the pace would continue. Church and school activities, Scouts and Brownies, car pooling and the boys' paper routes more than kept her busy. She was the day-laborer, the rule-maker and enforcer, the ever-available errand runner mired in the routine tasks of homemaking.

During those early, formative years I helped with the cooking, the dishes, the bedtime stories and evening prayers. Sometimes I would play catch and touch football with the boys after school and help Phyllis with the taxiing and paper routes as I could. But, things began to change. I was gone more than I was at home, and, when there, I was preoccupied. What were the tasks left undone? Who were the people I needed to see? What about this problem? What about that crisis? I took myself far too seriously. There were few days off, and no vacations until the older youngsters were in their teens.

As the pressures mounted Phyllis and I grew apart. Her parents had had a stormy, tempestuous relationship; their home had been an emotional jungle. Little in her background prepared her for the life she was called upon to live as a minister's wife. We enjoyed occasional times of warmhearted togetherness, but, more often than not, tension and misunderstanding ruled the day.

I have a host of memories related to my early years as a parish priest, memories related to Phyllis and the children. Many of them are warm and good, woven through with loving episodes. But there are also memories of dread and anger, of frustration and pain, of neglect and depression, and of sinful self-centeredness.

I pray those who read these words will take them to heart. (They are why I have made them the opening words of these shared memories.) My inadequacies as a husband and a father amounted to more than being "unfaithful" (as my resignation statement phrased it). Infidelity is an all-too-common sin. But, *when a partner undermines his or her partner's self-regard, when words of affirmation and commendation are withheld, when insensitivity and indifference prevail, when we become so centered in our own worlds that those about us are caused to suffer, an equally grave sin is committed.*

Phyllis was a lissome, attractive girl. She became a beautiful, charming and desirable woman. Although emotionally fragile she was a good person who genuinely cared about people. Her basic instincts and impressions were uncannily accurate. Had I been less driven and more attentive, less self-centered and more concerned about the well-being of my loved ones, how different the story might have been. My workaholic busyness denied my family and me those varied and wholesome activities and experiences that are requisite if family life is to be nurtured and covenantal bonds are to be strengthened. The tragedy is that words like these could be written by countless professional people, merchants, tradespeople, and increasingly, by women as well as men.

In March of 1984, after more than 40 years of marriage, Phyllis filed for divorce. After the suit was filed we spent a difficult year in Washington, D.C., thinking we might be able to work things out. It was not to be. Phyllis returned to Florida and I headed westward, bound for Denver where I would teach for the next six years. After long months the divorce was finalized.

One day Carlyle Marney, that marvelous, grizzly, renegade Southern Baptist preacher, and I were sitting on the steps of a ramshackle building at the Massanetta Springs campground in Virginia talking about our families, our work, and – of all things – the Council of Bishops of the United Methodist Church. "Jim," he said, "those old boys need to understand that the word 'bishop' is a verb and not a noun." Our titles and job descriptions define what we do, not who we are. And, who we are is vastly more important than what we do. Who we are, not what we do, shapes the most intimate and demanding relationships of our lives – and if we fail here we have failed.

CHAPTER II

"IF I HAD A THOUSAND LIVES TO LIVE"

Two people loved me blindly and without reservation, my mother and P.M. Boyd. Dr. Boyd was the pastor who received Phyllis and me into his church when we came to Florida in 1944. Later he led me into the ministry. He was the Methodist District Superintendent who appointed me to my first church as a college student, and his signature is affixed to the License to Preach that hangs on my workroom wall. When my father died Boyd wrote, "I can never take the place of your own father, but I could never be more devoted to you or take more pride in your ministry if you were my own son."

When I graduated from seminary I became Boyd's associate pastor at the First Methodist Church of Jacksonville, Florida, and for three years learned more about authentic ministry from him than I had in all my years of formal training. In 1968, when I was consecrated a bishop, he traveled to Peoria, Illinois, and joined five United Methodist bishops and my dear friend, Ben Garrison, in placing his great hand on my head to link me with those who had gone before. He died October 5, 1975, at the age of 86. At his funeral I said that though others had participated in the consecration ceremony in Peoria "it was Dick Boyd's hand that, for me, provided the 'apostolic succession'."

We corresponded at least once a month for more than twenty years. My first book, *The Journey That Men Make* (the title, a quotation from a James Michener novel, was inexcusably sexist even in 1969), was dedicated to him. When he received an advance copy he said he read the tribute and "could not keep the tears from streaming down (his) cheeks." He spoke of the "privilege of walking part of the journey with (me) – flesh of my flesh, blood of my blood, bone of my bone, soul of my soul." We often disagreed about matters political and theological and about what the church ought to be and do, our priorities and emphases were quite different, yet our love for one another is one of the abiding treasures of my life.

If I heard him say it once I heard him say it a hundred times: "If I had a thousand lives to live I would give them all to the ministry." Not me. When I was a small boy I dreamed of growing up to be a fireman, a locomotive engineer or an airplane pilot. (I must have read *The Red Eagle* a half dozen times before I was ten years old.) Later I would be drawn to public service, to teaching, industrial relations and art. (I won a national art contest of some sort when in high school and had a chance to work for Walt Disney. I later came to admire the late Herblock, the political cartoonist, and coveted his skills and influence.) Of necessity, as a very young father, I was a construction worker, a truck driver, a warehouse foreman and a clerk-typist in an office. After joining a conflict resolution firm in Washington, D.C. in 1985, I was told I would have made "a whale of a CIA agent." Frankly, that thought never entered my mind.

Boyd said if he had a thousand lives to live he would give them all to the ministry. Again – not me. I have never regretted entering the ministry, have found my deepest friendships in the life of the church, and it has offered me degrees of satisfaction and fulfillment I would never have dreamed possible as a young man. But in today's world there are so many choices to be made and paths to follow. Dreams and energies can be harnessed to any number of worthy callings, causes and opportunities. Faith is expressed and values are served in realms far removed from the world of organized religion.

Years ago I was in India conducting a series of conferences with a missionary friend. In Hyderabad I met S.P. Raju, an engineer and civil servant of the Indian government. He invented a smokeless *chula,* an oven intended to bring relative cleanliness to homes in Indian villages. He designed a one-room house that some felt could revolutionize village life. During the course of our conversation he handed me a tattered paper on which he had paraphrased the words of the apostle Paul:

> Raju...called to be an engineer, separated unto the Gospel of God in the evangelism of irrigation research for growing more food and bringing redemption from hunger...Also separated unto the Gospel of God in the evangelism and housing research for the poor, for bringing preventive redemption to them from congestion, dirt and disease, which are the potential sources of moral evil and sin.

Today there are countless secular voices that would never cite St. Paul, nor would they be caught dead using Raju's religious verbiage. Nonetheless, they reflect the same kind of selfless commitment speaking out on behalf of human rights, environmental issues and the health and well-being of persons. Ministry is not limited to the ordained, nor is it confined to those who find meaning and security in a particular belief system.

Why then did I turn toward the Christian ministry? True, it was in my genes. My father and grandfather had both been Methodist ministers. But, as most teens do, I had gone through my rebellious stages. I had rejected any thought of following in my father's footsteps. As a boy I had accompanied Dad to Taylor University in Indiana where he was to speak. I was perched on the platform with him (probably so that he could better control me). As he was being introduced I was asked if I would be a preacher when I grew up. "Absolutely not," I almost shouted. Time would change all that.

In 1945, when barely 20, I was an administrative assistant at the Army Air Force's Drew Field in Tampa, Florida. World War II was drawing to a close and my plans were uncertain. I didn't know how I wanted to shape my future. I was given an opportunity to move to the Civil Service Regional Office in Atlanta. That was considered quite an honor for one my age. My commanding officer at Drew was a Harvard graduate. He wanted me to go to the Harvard Business School and would try to wangle some sort of scholarship for me. Or, I could return to southern California and accept a scholarship at Redlands University. The options were there and one thing seemed obvious – even with a wife and two babies, further education was required.

THE "CALL"

At the time Phyllis and I lived in St. Petersburg. We had neighbors who attended an independent Presbyterian church that prided itself on being "evangelical, fundamental and premillenial." We went with them to Bible and missionary conferences while attending Dr. Boyd's church downtown. The sort of spiritual restlessness St. Augustine wrote about seemed to be stirring within me. One night Phyllis and I returned from a meeting at the nearby Presbyterian church and talked far into the night. We prayed – and made our decision to enter the ministry.

The next day I called Dr. Boyd and told him of our decision. He came to our home and talked to us about student scholarships available at Florida Southern College and about the possibility of serving a local church as a "student supply." That would make it possible to test the waters while putting food on our table. Before he left we stood in the center of our tiny living room with arms around each other as he led us in a prayer of dedication. God seemed very real, Christ was moving toward the center of our lives, and the church seemed to be both the logical next step and our final destination.

It was apparent from the outset that the Methodist Church in Florida was *southern* Methodist. It prided itself on being both evangelical and evangelistic. It had "revivals" and "camp meetings," stressed personal religious experience, and although somewhat more open (the word "liberal" would not apply) than its Southern Baptist neighbor, it was still a bastion of social, economic and religious conservatism. I was uncomfortable with many of its forms and decried its racism (in the 1940s the region was rigidly, cruelly segregated, as were its churches), but it was the church of my denominational heritage and the church to which I had returned. Dr. Boyd stood by to gently and persuasively show the way.

What was my motivation? I can't be sure. There was no voice from on high. My youth had been spent in southern California, a far more liberal region, and I had heard the likes of Gerald Kennedy, then in Palo Alto, later a bishop of the church. I had read *Das Kapital,* Ida Tarbell and Upton Sinclair (lest you think my reading was lop-sided, I also requested and received a copy of Hitler's *Mein Kampf* for my 16th birthday), and had been influenced by FDR's New Deal (my father was a chaplain in the Civilian Conservation Corps). I saw the church, though an imperfect and self-serving institution, as an agent of change. Seeds sown in my parents' home and at summer youth camps in the California mountains were beginning to sprout in the Deep South.

Other, subtle influences, some beyond my conscious awareness, were at work as well. Going through my father's papers at the time of his death I came upon an entry he had made in his diary the day following my birth:

> Today I am a supremely happy man. I have a wonderful wife, a lovely daughter, and now a son. He must be good as his mother is good, pure as I hope his sister will be, and the third preacher, God willing and calling. But, whatever he turns out to be he must have a character invincible to evil. May God make me worthy of this new charge.

I am certain my parents' influence played a role in my decision. But, "a character invincible to evil?" How crushed they would have been in 1983.

After our St. Petersburg decision was made I quit my job at Drew Field and began a cram course, digesting the books required by my denomination for the mandatory License to Preach. A year's study was crowded into a month. On May 10, 1945, I drove to Tampa and met with the District Licensing Committee. The men (and they were all men) were pleasant but almost indifferent, anxious to be on their ways, and I was offended. I had worked so hard, learned so much (I thought), and they dismissed me with a handful of cursory questions, a bit of cheerful chatter – and the coveted License. Less than a month later I preached my first sermon from the pulpit of the Methodist church in New Port Richey, the small frame church to which I had been appointed.

NEW PORT RICHEY AND FLORIDA SOUTHERN

The churches I served and the schools I attended were intertwined during the early years of my ministry. The four years we spent in New Port Richey ran parallel to my years at Florida Southern College. Florida Southern was in Lakeland, 60 miles from New Port Richey. If my 1936 Ford was in running condition it got me there. Otherwise I hitchhiked or took a bus. I attended the "Community College" – a Friday night/all day Saturday program designed primarily for school teachers. It served my purposes but was far from an academic challenge. The Floridan Hotel always had a $1. room for me if I had a dollar. If I didn't, which was often the case, I'd pull onto a dimly lit street and sleep in the back seat of my car. My weekend meal was shrimp creole for 90 cents. I confess, when I hear students today haggling over perks, comforts and benefits, I'm tempted to react like the old fogy I am becoming. "Why, when I was your age," I'd like to say, "we knew what it meant to work and sacrifice, yada, yada, yada..." but I bite my tongue and internalize my impatience with them.

My time at Southern was surprisingly fruitful. I spent long

hours with the college president, a colorful, brilliant, eccentric disciple of John Dewey and friend of Frank Lloyd Wright, and with Charles Thrift, his stolid, well-trained vice president. The two men offered me "learning-through-encounter" credits, assigning books to be read, concepts to grapple with and be explored, and the equivalent of oral examinations. They had earned their Ph.D.s at the University of Chicago and said their methods were perfectly consistent with what they had experienced there. Later I would find nothing quite that slack-jawed and permissive during my graduate studies at Chicago, but I didn't complain at the time.

There were others: a history professor who thought we ought to preempt the Soviets and drop an A-bomb on the Kremlin; a 90-year-old professor of Greek and New Testament who quietly, with a saintly demeanor, told us that the Lord's Prayer was the only prayer he prayed; a Scottish professor of philosophy who had a white goatee and a brogue straight from Glasgow. There was a frail teacher of English Literature who trembled with emotion when she read Shakespeare's works aloud, and a Speech teacher who looked like a Russian countess.

And there was Grace de Casterline. She had studied under Shirley Jackson Case at Chicago. Fresh from her doctoral studies, a bit unsure of herself and not much of a scholar, she was one of the finest instructors I ever had. She involved us, interacted with us, challenged us, smilingly took some of our crude notions to task, and appeared willing to listen to us and even learn from us.

Years later when some vigilante conservative clergy demanded that President Spivey dismiss her because of her "modernism," he called some of us and asked us to help marshal support for her. We did – and her faculty position was made secure.

In 1985, years after her retirement, I visited Grace in a North Carolina retirement home near Asheville. Nearly blind, her voice almost gone, she taught a Bible class for residents every week. We walked through the hallways arm in arm as she described her life there and greeted her friends and "students." Proud of her liberating role as their teacher she would nudge me and say, "He's a Unitarian...She's a Unitarian...He's a Unitarian." A teacher to the end she was convinced she had led them to a more reasonable faith.

On October 12, 1993, after being unaware of the world around her for more than two years, she died in a Virginia health care center at the age of 92. Two weeks later I led her memorial service in the Danforth Chapel on the Florida Southern campus. I read from the 8th Psalm, from Amos and Ecclesiastes, from First Corinthians 13 and the Sermon on the Mount, all passages she had breathed life into in the classroom decades before. I also read some of her poetry that typified the richness and beauty of her spirit. This is one of the verses I read:

> There's a star above the valley
> And the trees are all aflame,
> While the heart of earth is breaking with a cry
> For the aching, thrilling beauty
> Of the autumn's solemn pageant,
> As the glory of the Lord is passing by.
>
> O, the cleansing, fiery grandeur
> Of October's haunting splendor,
> When God drops His rainbow mantle from on high!
> Then the stars of Love, resplendent,
> Fill the reverent soul with wonder
> Like a tall and crimson taper in life's sky.

During the drudgery of my less-than-ideal days at Florida Southern College, Grace de Casterline, more than anyone else, made the hardships of my undergraduate studies not only endurable, but informative and enjoyable.

While at Southern I was introduced to the tortured Russian novelist, Fyodor Dostoevsky, in a literature class. My life would never be the same. *Crime and Punishment* was only the beginning. *The Brothers Karamazov* with its "legend of the Grand

Inquisitor" came next, followed by *The Possessed, The Idiot, A Raw Youth, Notes from Underground,* and his *Diary,* biographies and monographs. I immersed myself in the writer's dark and morbid world view. (I now teach a course on "Dostoevsky and Pastoral Psychology" to seminary students.)

Whether writing his first novel, *Poor Folks,* or *The Brothers Karamazov* 35 years later, whether describing the human condition or exploring "the God question" that always haunted him, Dostoevsky wrote out of the seething depths of his own soul. Stefan Zweig said "he kiss(ed) the cross with fever parched lips."(1) Later I would study Barth, Brunner, and Reinhold Niebuhr as they dealt with human nature, but they added not one whit to my understanding of the shadow-side, the proud, self-worshiping, murky side of each of us. Theologians tend to reduce things to neat, structured, systematic categories. Dostoevsky was not at home with dogmatic schemes and rigid structures. Rather, he saw "passionate agitation (as the) radical characteristic of human nature."(2) As I have counseled with parishioners and clients across the years, and as I have come to learn more about myself, I believe he was closer to the truth than many of the thinkers seminarians are exposed to.

When Phyllis and I were at Menninger's diagnostic clinic late in 1983, a burly, insightful psychiatrist and I explored the meaning of *Crime and Punishment's* student, Raskolnikov. Raskolnikov's Napoleonic musings, despicable crime, personal disintegration, flight away from responsibility, and love for the prostitute, Sonya, that led to his Siberian "katorga" (cleansing), were central to the story. Rightly or wrongly, the psychiatrist attached significance to my fascination with Raskolnikov and his subconscious desire to "get caught."

Another 19th century figure who entered my life during my New Port Richey/ Florida Southern years was Robertson of Brighton. I came upon Frederick W. Robertson in a used bookstore. All five volumes of his sermons had been condensed into one 840-page book that sold for $1.50. Not knowing Robertson from Adam, but knowing a bargain when I saw one, I made the purchase. That book became the basis of my devotional life for two years. And, those sermons opened other doors: James Blackwood's, *The Soul of Frederick W. Robertson,* and his letters as well as other biographies. Robertson, like Dostoevsky, possessed not only a brilliant mind, but a brooding spirit.

Robertson's health was fragile. His marriage was far from ideal. Though of high birth he identified with the working class of Brighton and was ostracized by his critics. Because of his open, probing views of Scripture and doctrine he was labeled a heretic. He knew sorrow, depression and solitude, but believed in the cleansing, healing power of suffering and grace. His unorthodox ministry in a relatively obscure parish came to an end when he died of a brain tumor at 37.

His sermon topics revealed the man: "The Doubt of Thomas," "The Power of Sorrow," "The Transitoriness of Life," "Religious Depression," "The Illusiveness of Life," "Christian Progress by Oblivion of the Past," and the most well-known and self-revealing of them all, "The Loneliness of Christ." Imagine this youthful, slender man leaning toward his congregation, reaching into the souls of his parishioners, saying in his resonant tones, "You are tried alone – alone you must pass into the desert – alone you must bear and conquer the agony – alone you must be sifted by the world." But, he didn't stop there. He concluded his message by saying, "God is near you. Throw yourself fearlessly upon him. Trembling mortal that you are, there is an unknown might within your spirit which will wake when you command it...Let his strength be yours...The Father is with you. Look to him and he will save you." There was a timelessness about him that touches and moves us even today.

The Norman Vincent Peales and Robert Shullers, the sunshine offerings of "possibility thinking" and the multi-faceted, intellectual pablum promoted by jazzed-up "contemporary" services in today's mega-churches, leave me cold. They reach people; without doubt they help some people; but, they tend to offer religion without a cross. Unless our various forms of moral and spiritual illness and death are acknowledged and grappled with, resurrection becomes myth without meaning.

From the beginning I resented the circumstances surrounding my marriage to Phyllis. I didn't understand the tugs of war that pulled me in contrary directions. Preoccupied with my own frustrations and inner warfare I failed to realize what a price Phyllis was paying, how insecure and troubled she was, and how hard she was trying. I felt drawn to the Dostoevskys and Robertsons, the Van Goghs and Rodins, the D.H. Lawrences and Hemingways, but I didn't move beyond the bleakness of their personal worlds. I preached about accountability, compassion and other-centered love, but I didn't offer them to those closest to me. Aware of my own "suffering," the absence of "happiness" in my life, I was hurting those closest to me by my self-centered insensitivity. My words were denied by my moods and actions.

In all honesty, at that juncture it was neither my family nor my schooling that was the center of my life, it was the New Port Richey church. When we arrived in 1945 the church claimed 150 members. Now, more than 50 years later, I can name nearly half of them: St. Clair, Baker, Mount, Mayer, Swartsel, Keller, Coble, McIntyre, Potter, Pierce – the list could go on. There is a special mystique about the first church a young minister serves, but New Port Richey was different. Its warm and uncritical acceptance of a young, untrained couple set a tone for those formative years. Its practical faithfulness, ministry to indigent families, cottage prayer meetings, its eager participation in the Meals for Millions program following World War II, and the joy it demonstrated in virtually everything it did, underscored the meaning of Christian community in a local setting. New Port Richey is more than a hundred miles from where we now live, but at least once a year I drive across the state, retrace steps taken more than half a century ago and gratefully remember.

Palmetto came next, but it was not the same. It had a contingent of "holiness," "second-blessing," self-styled saints who took it upon themselves to either humble their young parson or bring him around to their point of view and level of perfection. There were some good and thoughtful people in that congregation, but they seemed to be outnumbered by the cantankerous and mean-spirited. In 1982, Phyllis and I flew down from Indianapolis to help the church celebrate its 100th anniversary. The members presented themselves with a plaque listing the 55 pastors who had served them over their century-long existence. They seemed proud of the turnover rate revealed by the plaque. I couldn't say a word because we lasted no longer than our predecessors. After a year and with a brand new baby we headed for Atlanta and seminary.

OAK GROVE AND SEMINARY

Just as Florida Southern and New Port Richey are linked together in my mind, so too are the Oak Grove Methodist Church and the Candler School of Theology. It would have been great to attend Union, Yale or Princeton. Their faculties in the early '50s were the *creme de la creme* of Christian thought. But Candler, on the campus of Emory University in Atlanta, accepted me where I was and provided a stimulating learning environment. Today it is recognized as one of the finest schools of theology in the nation.

The faculty in 1950 presented an interesting mix of opinions and personalities. There was W.A. Smart ("Old Marblehead" we called him) who breathed life into the Hebrew prophets. Mack Stokes was a blend of Borden Parker Bowne personalism and Asbury's conservative religiosity. As the years passed Asbury won out. In his classes he railed against the "tradition of passivity" in the church, yet later, as a bishop in Mississippi, he championed that very tradition as he tried to safeguard the racial status quo by establishing a "Jim Crow" district.

Claude Thompson was a soft-spoken Wesleyan scholar who, with his family, attended Oak Grove. He played a mean second base on the seminary softball team (I was the catcher). G. Ray Jordan, who taught homiletics, was a feisty master-sergeant type with impressive skills and credentials. William R. Cannon was a gifted church historian, a spellbinding lecturer and a colorful human being. Elected to the episcopal office in 1968, he became a key figure in both the World Methodist Council and in Roman Catholic/Methodist dialogue efforts. His autobiography, *A Magnificent Obsession,* published shortly before his death in 1997, reflected his brilliance, his passionate devotion to tradition, the scope of his influence, and his monumental ego. When my father died Cannon was the one faculty member who took me aside and provided a tender pastoral presence.

Odd Hagen and Gordon Rupp, visiting imports from Scandinavia and England, brought "continental theology" and a British brand of Wesleyan thought to our campus. They visited us in our home, ate with us, shared with us without a trace of condescension, and introduced us to realms of thought far beyond the parochial limits of the Deep South.

While in seminary I held revivals and preaching missions, spoke on college campuses and at youth assemblies, and gave motivational talks for an insurance company's staff managers' training schools. I exceeded the maximum number of "allowed absences" each term – but there were four little mouths to feed. Even so, I finished in two years with both Stokes and Thompson urging me to continue my studies, earn a Ph.D., and teach. I chose to return to the local parish.

Oak Grove had prospered during my brief ministry there. Working with five other seminarians over the two-year period we received more than 100 members, upped the budget significantly, and prepared the church to move from the status of a "student appointment" to a "charge." Today Oak Grove has more than 2000 members and boasts one of the largest Church Schools in the Atlanta area.

THE SUNSHINE STATE

When I graduated Dr. Boyd asked me to return to Florida and become his associate pastor at First Church, Jacksonville. I didn't want to. I had already served three churches and felt more than ready to move out on my own. Yet, I owed Boyd so much. I was genuinely devoted to him, had no need to declare my independence, and had no difficulty in recognizing in him a worthy authority figure. So, the die was cast. The young Armstrongs headed for Jacksonville and for three of the most delightful and meaningful years we would ever experience.

Boyd was a complex human being. He was the manager/therapist Robert Bellah described in *Habits of the Heart*.(3) He was an administrator par excellence. He rose at the crack of dawn each morning, went to his office and got "his ducks in a row" (as he used to say), organizing his activities for the day. As the day progressed he would check each item off. Deeply involved in the affairs of Florida Methodism and the city of Jacksonville he chaired committees, sat on boards and ordered the affairs of the church he served. He touched more bases and interacted with more people, one on one, in the course of a typical day than anyone I have ever known.

He was a superb pastor. Each year we divided the membership of the church (about 1500) down the middle and visited in every home in the parish. We divided hospital calls. His were models of meaningful brevity with no needless tarrying and no idle chatter; just genuine concern. He was as strait-laced in his habits (apart from an occasional off-color joke) as a person could be. Yet, he seemed shockproof. No human frailty caught him off guard. His capacity to be one with the errant youth, the grieving widow, the broken and discredited public official, or the foul-smelling panhandler was almost beyond belief.

Beyond his professional disciplines and shepherding instincts was his utter unselfishness. During my three years at First Church I preached as often as he did (we had Sunday morning and evening services). He permitted and encouraged me to develop a television ministry, provide statewide leadership for the Methodist youth fellowship, assume ecumenical responsibilities, and become involved in community affairs (as often as not controversial). More than once I heard him say, as he took sinful liberty with Scripture, "I must decrease that you might increase." Academic training is designed to equip the mind and provide professional tools. It does not necessarily nurture healthy attitudes, accentuate natural gifts and feed the human spirit. P.M. Boyd did those things and much, much more.

As I think of the staff people with whom I have worked – Jim Jenkins, Lester Bill, Larry Curtis, Russell Dilley, Robert Paul, Jim Pomeroy, Ron Hartung, Rueben Job, Norm Shawchuck, Kathy Trotter, Bruce Ough, Jim Steele, and most recently, my associate and later co-pastor, Jana Norman-Richardson (who, barely 30, was named one of two Assistant Moderators of the United Church of Christ), I am mindful of the tremendous contributions they made to my ministry. I tried to surround myself with strength knowing that if persons are encouraged to seize initiatives and are given the freedom to cultivate and demonstrate their skills, they will not only strengthen the church, they will bring credit to themselves and to those who are considered accountable for their labors. If I was able to build and work with able staffs it was due, in no small measure, to Boyd's example.

When Dr. Boyd was named superintendent of the Miami District in 1955, First Church Jacksonville asked the resident bishop to appoint me to succeed Boyd as their senior minister. Bishop Branscomb said there was no precedent for such an appointment. Boyd, who wanted me to succeed him, was deeply disappointed, especially when I was named to serve the Methodist church in Vero Beach. Feeling that I needed to be tried and tested in a more demanding situation he muttered, "Brother Jim, you can stand in one corner of that town and pee right across it." That was neither fair to the good bishop nor to a delightful community.

Vero Beach was great for our family. The youngsters enjoyed the beach and school activities. The Dodgers, then the *Brooklyn* Dodgers, had their spring training camp there. Carl Erskine, their ace pitcher, attended our church regularly, and Peewee Reese and Gil Hodges came occasionally. Erskine even took our son John fishing a time or two. Phyllis and I made new friends and embraced a more relaxed life style. And, I was able to take advantage of the more leisurely pace of the beach community and pursue graduate studies at Boston University and the University of Chicago.

GRADUATE SCHOOLS, CARL ROGERS AND PASTORAL COUNSELING

Phyllis joined me my first summer in Boston. We had a rickety apartment overlooking the Charles River, took long walks and weekend drives delving into the riches of New England, listened to the Boston Pops orchestra in their open-air concerts, and spent uncharacteristic but valued time together. The next summer we had a brand new baby so I took the two oldest youngsters with me. We cooked for ourselves and cleaned our own digs. We roamed the countryside each weekend from Lexington and Concord to Plymouth and the coast of Maine. Some evenings I would slip out and listen to the McCarthy hearings at a neighborhood bar.

While at B.U. I studied with Paul Johnson. He was a gentle, perceptive, well-trained scholar. My first published work appeared in his book, *Personality and Religion*.(4) The chapter, "Jeanne Andrews," was a psycho-biography of Phyllis I had written for one of his classes. Johnson would make frequent reference to Carl Rogers, then at the peak of his career at the University of Chicago. Why not get it straight from the horse's mouth? I went to Chicago.

Rogers of "client-centered therapy" fame was the most impressive and consistent person with whom I ever studied. In 1956-57 he was preparing to leave the University of Chicago for an ill-fated attempt to bring psychologists and psychiatrists together for joint training and research projects at the University of Wisconsin. Later he would help shape the encounter group movement from La Jolla, California.

Whether I was in the Rogers' home with Carl and his wife Helen, or experienced him in a classroom or on a training film, in a counseling session or simply engaged him in casual conversation, he always reflected the same gentle strength, the same unique regard for persons, the same gift for listening and the same commitment to persons "in the process of becoming," that is communicated in his written work. In a helpful biological study a former colleague is quoted as saying:

> He is a man who has continued to grow, to discover himself, to test himself, to be genuine, to review his experience, to learn from it...to stand for something, to live honestly (and) fully, in the best human sense.(5)

Carl Rogers incarnated the traits of the "fully functioning person" he wrote about. He was an authentic guru from whom the helping professions continue to have so much to learn.

Why did I pursue graduate studies in the field of psychotherapy? Maybe I tilted in that direction because of my earlier immersion in Dostoevsky, Robertson and some of the others. After all, Freud said he gained many of his insights from Dostoevsky. I realized that my studies at Candler had been wanting in this area. My own internal struggles made me realize how much I needed to learn about myself and those about me. Even more important, I felt ill-equipped to deal with the personal and relational crises that were beating a constant pathway to my study door. Too often well-intentioned counselors, without adequate training or lacking personal stability, damage the wounded and troubled souls who turn to them for help.

Quite apart from my studies the church kept me more than busy. We employed an associate pastor and had a vigorous youth program. Three services each Sunday required thoughtful preparation. During my three years in Vero the membership grew from 780 to 1320, and we were instrumental in "planting" two new churches, Christ-by-the-Sea (today it has about 700 members) and Asbury (it has some 350).

In 1945, at the tender age of 20, I had been a "new Christian." My commitment to Christ and the church was genuine. I had no objectified professional ambitions, no success-oriented goals in mind. I simply wanted to be faithful assuming everything else would fall into place.

Thirteen years later, with college, seminary and graduate studies behind me, and with more than a decade of pastoral experience under my belt, I had changed. My commitment to ministry was still there, not as romantic as before, but intact. While I had grown more impatient with my denomination and the church as an institution, I had grown more patient with and accepting of human failings. I continued to be restless, discontented with much in my personal world, but new doors were opening.

BROADWAY, INDIANAPOLIS

In May of 1958, we were "called" to the Broadway Methodist Church in Indianapolis. The process was far more "congregational" than "episcopal." People from the church had come to Vero to hear me. Phyllis and I had flown to Indianapolis to be interviewed. Bishop and Mrs. Richard C. Raines (he was the presiding bishop in Indiana) had visited Florida, attended our church (because of the crowd they were stashed, unnoticed, in the narthex), and talked with us. There had been a national search and the pointer had swung in our direction. I was young but felt ready.

Broadway is a huge Gothic structure on Fall Creek Parkway just two and a half miles from the center of the city. It serves the larger metropolitan area, but its immediate neighborhood, on the edge of the inner city, was changing. In 1958, with more than 3300 members, it was the largest Methodist church in the state.

I succeeded Robert Bruce Pierce who went from Broadway to Metropolitan in Detroit and later served Chicago's Methodist Temple in the heart of the loop. He had been at Broadway nine years, was extremely popular, had taken hundreds of new members into the church and would be a hard act to follow.

At Broadway preaching would have to be central. My

emphases would be different from those of Bob Pierce. He was relatively conservative and cautious. I was not. He was a Republican serving a Republican congregation in a Dixiecrat/Republican city. I would not be. He courted the business community and was embraced by it. I didn't see myself in that role. My preaching would have to be biblical, faithful to tradition without being bound by it, responsive to the needs of the people, and applicable to a world beyond the boundaries of the church and the city.

I determined to balance my preaching. There would be a series of sermons on the Hebrew prophets followed by one on contemporary "isms." There would be series on the parables, on prayer, on the sins of society, and on the Sermon on the Mount. I preferred preaching in series for the sake of thought and theme development.

I seldom preached single-issue sermons. There were exceptions. In the light of the Supreme Court's decision on prayer in public schools I praised the propriety of that decision. With the "wall of separation" being challenged today as never before by the fulminations of the religious right, by the posting of religious symbols in public buildings, by voucher systems and George W. Bush's faith-based initiatives, it continues to be imperative that thoughtful voices address the issues at stake in the separation of church and state.

With the House Un-American Activities Committee riding high in the saddle I felt impelled to preach on "The Communist Lie," while underscoring the importance of our First Amendment rights and civil liberties. The John Birch Society was born in Indianapolis in 1958, the year of my arrival there, and on October 10, 1965, I preached on "The John Birch Mentality and the Church." More than 3000 copies of that one were mailed out in response to requests.

Although I made frequent reference to racial issues and was deeply involved in the civil rights movement I preached only one sermon, "Long Minutes," dealing exclusively with black-white relations and racial justice. Later it would be reprinted in *The Pulpit Speaks on Race,*(6) along with sermons by

Eugene Carson Blake, Martin Luther King, Jr., Carlyle Marney and others. It was my first inclusion in a volume like that and I was sinfully proud.

The Sunday following JFK's assassination I preached about that. The same thing was true after the MLK killing, and the region-wide memorial service for Dr. King was held in our overflowing church. I spoke at that, too. Certain events require homiletical response.

My Indianapolis ministry was seen by some as controversial. After all, it was the '60s. Who had a right to stay out of the fray? Even so, my preaching was basically pastoral. Typical topics: "In the Shadows Unafraid," "When the Skies Grow Dark," "For Those Who Worry Too Much," "When the Going Gets Rough," "For Those Who Try Too Hard," and "On Being Fair To Ourselves." I didn't follow the Lectionary in those days. When I returned to the parish ministry in 1991, I followed it faithfully if not slavishly. The Lectionary provides a built-in balance. Those who insist that it doesn't provide sufficient latitude for creative thinking and prophetic preaching don't know what they are talking about.

I am committed to the importance of *pastoral* preaching (another reason why psychological studies and disciplines are important for clergy)! Following my resignation in 1983, I was in churches almost every Sunday. I heard the man reputed to be the most effective biblical preacher in Manhattan. I heard Ft. Lauderdale's answer to Robert Shuller (although James Kennedy has more in common with Pat Robertson than with Dr. Shuller). I was in Presbyterian, Congregational, Methodist, Episcopal and Unitarian churches. But, with the exception of David Rees in Miami and Bert Sikkolee (who had been through a recent divorce) in Alexandria, Virginia, not one of them spoke to the ache and yearning of my soul. It may have been the roll of the dice. It may have been my spiritual state. But, at that stage of my voyage I was a seeker who was left adrift because of the boring irrelevance of pulpit after pulpit. I emerged from those painful months convinced that *no matter how profound and correct the theology, no matter how accurate and uncanny the insight into current events, no matter how sound the biblical interpretation and skilled the exegesis, no matter how clever the phrases and compelling the style, if we do not speak to the troubled, restless spirits of our hearers, offering them words of understanding, acceptance, forgiveness and grace, we have failed both them and the gospel we have been called to proclaim.*

Harry Emerson Fosdick called preaching "group therapy." Roy Burkhart said that following his Sunday morning sermons at First Community in Columbus, Ohio, listeners would cluster around him asking for further conversation. The minister, because of his or her role, will be called upon to counsel. Sensitive and perceptive preaching amplifies both needs and opportunities. It encourages self-examination, offers fresh insight and awareness, stirs deep-seated emotions, explores inner resources, and highlights the desirability and central place of spiritual disciplines. More and more, my ministry at Broadway became a counseling ministry. There are risks and dangers involved.

We are tempted to play God. Too many "religious" counselors, armed with their understanding of the Bible and their firm moral convictions, assume they have an obligation to judge and direct, to tell those who turn to them for guidance what they "ought" to do and how they "ought" to function. In saying "do this" or "do that" they deny the autonomy and personal responsibility of the counselee. Counseling should not divorce itself from moral judgments, but those judgments need to be formed by the person seeking guidance. It is neither the place nor the right of the religious counselor – or any other therapist – to take over another person's life.

We are tempted to choose up sides. To hear only one voice or to be exposed to only one list of complaints does not present a whole picture. If brought into a domestic dispute I insist upon talking to both parties when possible, both individually and together. I tell them it is not my place to keep them together or to recommend separation, but to help them think through their respective needs and responsibilities. No outsider (and no matter how skilled, the counselor is an "outsider") can fully understand the subtleties and nuances of relationship.

We are sometimes tempted to over-identify with those who come to us, encouraging dependency or transference. It is one thing for a therapist and client to accept each other as friends, it is quite something else for a therapist to invest emotions in the well-being of another to the degree that objectivity is lost and professional competence is blurred. Counselors have their own blind spots and subjective needs. Failing to recognize them jeopardizes the counseling process. *If we sense we are moving into a situation we do not fully understand or if we become too deeply involved, it is our obligation to refer those who have come to us to other therapists or agencies with the required resources and abilities.*

There is the temptation to seduce. Clergy are as human as doctors and lawyers who live with this temptation on a daily basis. There were times at Broadway when I insisted on my study door being left open. I sometimes asked my secretary to join the counselee and me in the chapel for prayer. Sometimes it seemed advisable to refer the counselee to another member of the staff. The location of a chair, the touch of a hand, the verbalization of ambivalent feelings – these are the "little things" that can easily set the stage for the violation of confidence and trust. Recent volumes like *Ethics and Spiritual Care* by Lebacqz and Driskill,(7) *Sex in the Parish* by Lobacqz and Barton,(8) and *Clergy Malpractice* by Maloney and others,(9) underscore the importance of what I've been saying. *Lives can be irreparably scarred and ministry destroyed because naive, vulnerable or unprincipled clergy take advantage of those who turn to them for solace and guidance.*

The counseling encounter in the Protestant church can be the equivalent of the old Roman Catholic confessional. When a burdened soul, shattered by the knowledge of personal failure and haunted by guilt, turns to her or his minister, that minister, as an emissary of God, can speak the liberating words, "Your sins are forgiven." Those words and the acceptance of that forgiveness can free the human spirit and make possible new beginnings.

Confidentiality is of utmost importance in our preaching and counseling ministries. There is no graver breach of ethics in congregational life than the violation of confidences. Sermon illustrations should never betray circumstances or events shared with us in the privacy of confidential conversations. If we want to make reference to a conversation or event that could be helpful to others, we must *always* gain prior permission to use it. There are no exceptions. In the Dakotas I told the superintendents with whom I worked that they were, under no circumstances, to divulge confidences shared with them with their spouses. I inherited an Administrative Assistant in Indiana who had opened the bishop's mail to determine what should come to the bishop and what might be routed elsewhere. I told him I would open my own mail. What is written to one person is meant for that person's eyes only. A confidence is a sacred trust.

Having said all of this, Broadway was far more than a preaching place or a house of worship with counseling chambers. The church's logo, appearing on its bulletins, letterheads and publications, was and is a cross, a basin and a towel. We are called to be a servant church.

The October, 1967, issue of *Together,* Methodism's national magazine, featured an article on Broadway called, "The Church That Refuses To Die." It opened with the words, "What does a church do when it finds itself a white island in a black sea?" When I went to Broadway in 1958 its surroundings were white (the Mapleton-Fall Creek neighborhood was home to some 17,000 residents). When I left 10 years later it was 90% African-American.

The *Together* article reported a revealing incident in the life of the church. Louis Lomax, a well-known black writer and TV personality, had spoken at Broadway. During the course of his speech he turned to me and said, "People like you are running away from churches like this all over the country and we're taking them over. You've given us some of your finest churches."

Given an opportunity to reply I said, "My friend, we are not about to 'give' you this church. We'll share it with you. It can be ours together. But, we won't give it away." The article said that the largely Negro audience "applauded warmly."(10)

The writer described programs that were designed to serve both the church and the neighborhood. He spoke of small study and prayer groups that were meeting across the face of the parish, of outpost Sunday schools that reached nearly 200 children each week, of a Friday night Teen Canteen, a Thrift Shop, a health clinic, a well-baby clinic, a Planned Parenthood center, Head Start classes that utilized the space, an after-school program that featured remedial reading as well as sewing and cooking classes, Bible study and recreation – programs involving more than 400 elementary school children each week.

In 1969, Thomas J. Mullen wrote *The Dialogue Gap*, in which he described Broadway. "Only six years ago," he said, "Broadway...was called a cathedral with the largest congregation of its denomination in the state." Mullin described the "program modification" that followed the changing racial complexion of the neighborhood. "Instead of moving to the suburbs," he wrote, "the church, which had been known for its wealth, remained and became known for its service."(11) Rudiger Reitz, in *The Church in Experiment*, referred to Broadway's congregation as one noted not for its wild and radical experimentation, but for its willingness to renew the church from within and to transform the institutional structure through a smooth evolution." He called Broadway "one of the exemplary churches in America."(12)

Today Broadway is served by a Micronesian native of Guam, Frank Sablan. It went into a decline during the years following my departure. Over the next 30 years its membership dipped below 500 and, when Sablan went there in 1995, worship attendance had fallen to 140. However, many of the faithful had remained and commitment to diversity had stayed in place. Today worship attendance has more than doubled and it is one of the faster growing congregations in the city. More than 10% of its membership is black. A Korean congregation has become part of its church family. And, Broadway has become a haven for gay and lesbian Christians.

In spite of the ugly face United Methodism showed the rest of the world at its General Conference in Cleveland in May,

2000, as it debated the issues of homosexuality and same-sex unions, defeating a resolution that simply acknowledged that the church "has been unable to arrive at a common mind" on the thorny issue, Broadway is one of those prophetic congregations that continues to be on the cutting edge of vital, contemporary witness. Many of Broadway's committees are now chaired by gays or lesbians who, along with African-American congregants, have assumed positions of leadership.

I return to Broadway every year or two to be with family members. Our daughter, Terri, and her daughter Phyllis, and son-in-law, Rob, are in the church. Phyllis is an attorney for the state of Indiana, and Rob is vice principal of an Indianapolis high school. Both are active in the neighborhood program (and play on the church's softball team). When I go back I am able, in some degree, to re-experience the glory days of the '60s. Those ten years at Broadway represent, for me, the promise and relative actualization of a community of faith, located in the heart of a metropolis, strategically situated in a troubled, rapidly changing neighborhood, being what it is called to be and doing what it is called to do.

...WITH MORE TO COME

In July, 1968, I was elected a bishop of the United Methodist Church, the only bishop elected that year in the North Central Jurisdiction. The Sunday morning of my consecration, before leaving for the First Methodist Church of Peoria where Dr. Boyd and Ben Garrison would join the bishops in the traditional laying-on of hands, I slipped into the hotel bathroom, leaned against the door, and for one fleeting moment, wept. This was not how I had envisioned my future. I had no desire to turn away from the claims of my church, but I was leaving the parish ministry, a ministry I knew and loved. I was leaving a servant church that had grown to national prominence, and I was leaving a wonderful group of friends and co-workers who had made that growth and those servant ministries possible. And I was moving into a strange, uncharted future.

CHAPTER III

"YOU AIN'T FIT TO BE NO METHODIST PREACHER"

I would not have been elected to the episcopacy in any year other than 1968. It was a watershed year. In a sense the '60s ended with the chaotic Democratic Convention in Chicago. It was the decade of the civil rights movement, protest against an evil war in southeast Asia, the "new politics" and "the greening of America" – and I was a part of them. In normal times the church would have elected a more conventional type.

When I was elected an Indianapolis columnist wrote:

> Consider the prospects of a minister who uses the pulpit to speak of politics (as distinguished from partisan candidates)...
> Who himself identifies with partisan candidates and their causes...
> Who speaks freely in his pulpit of current, controversial issues and applies the judgment of the Gospel to them...
> Who, with church officials, opens the doors of a white church to Negroes and pridefully sees some of them proceed to the official board and commissions of the church and one to a higher council of the denomination...
> It seems reasonable that any minister who committed these "heresies" to white Protestant

tradition would either be thrown out on his ear – or made a bishop.

The Rev. A. James Armstrong, who did all of these things as the senior minister of the Broadway United Methodist Church, has been elected a bishop, at 43, the youngest of all United Methodist bishops.(1)

Up to this point I have discussed my family, my "calling," my schooling and the churches I served, the vital role of preaching, pastoral care and counseling, and servant ministries in the life of the congregation. None of these emphases should be pitted against social action. Activism, pastoral ministries and spiritual nurture are complimentary facets of the same inclusive gospel. Take any one of them away and the church is crippled; the gospel is betrayed.

In the summer of 1980, I was transferred from the Dakotas Area of the UMC to Indiana. The *Sioux Falls Argus Leader,* in a feature article, reported: "South Dakota's Social Conscience Prepares to Move On." A syndicated columnist called me, "America's most activist bishop." Doubtless an overstatement, but where did the reputation come from? What were the origins of my "social conscience?"

ORIGINS OF A SOCIAL CONSCIENCE

The instincts were there from the beginning. Before going to seminary I had worked for Senator Claude Pepper's reelection when he was confronted by the racist campaign of the attractive, urbane George Smathers. Early on I joined the Southern Regional Council, a moderate organization committed to racial justice, and the Southern Conference Educational Fund, headed by Jim Dombrowski and dubbed "subversive" by the Florida state legislature in the '50s. In Palmetto I preached from a black pulpit for the first time and felt a sweep of emotions I had not experienced before. Initially, justice for African-Americans was my "cause," but with the passage of time and exposure to a broader spectrum of need, my concerns embraced a wider range of issues.

During my years at Broadway I assumed my share of civic responsibilities. I was active in the Urban League, the Community Service Council and the Mayor's Progress Committee. Active in Democratic Party politics I went on statewide television to denounce the divisive candidacy of George Wallace during the '64 presidential primary. In 1967 I became vice chair of Hoosiers for Peace, and met with a group of fellow Hoosiers and Al Lowenstein in a bank basement, becoming a part of the "dump Johnson" movement. I was named vice chair of Hoosiers for a Democratic Alternative. In a series of feature articles the *Indianapolis News* named me one of the city's "movers and shakers."

My first assignment as a bishop was to the Dakotas Area (there were those who felt I was being banished to Siberia). Shortly after arriving in South Dakota I joined others in Pierre, the state capitol, to fight for the life of Thomas White Hawk, a young Native American who had brutally murdered a jeweler.

In 1969, I visited South Vietnam with a "study team on political and religious freedom." That trip became a defining moment as I saw how U.S. diplomats and military leaders could join in misrepresenting reality and deceiving fellow Americans.

Both delegates to the General Assembly of the World Council of Churches, Senator George McGovern and I first met in Uppsala, Sweden, in 1968. The senator and his wife Eleanor became close friends after our move to their home state. I actively supported him during his 1972 presidential bid and in his Senate race two years later.

In 1973, at the request of the National Council of Churches, I served as a mediator when the American Indian Movement (AIM) took hostages and seized the Pine Ridge Reservation village of Wounded Knee.

During my Dakota years (1968 to 1980) I appeared at congressional hearings, before legislative committees, and at press conferences, opposing capital punishment, condemning the Thieu-Ky regime in Saigon, supporting the recommendations of the Rome Food Conference, urging reconstruction aid for a war-torn Vietnam, pleading for handgun control, defending the rights of gays and lesbians, opposing a constitutional amendment that would prohibit abortion, and advocating a nuclear arms freeze. I guess I had become your classic "knee-jerk liberal."

During my years of episcopal leadership I gladly served four years as President of Methodism's General Board of Church and Society, and five years as Chair of the denomination's Commission on Religion and Race, thus expressing my commitment to social justice more formally.

But again, where did it all begin? How does one track the development of one's social conscience?

When I was growing up my father served small town churches in Indiana. The towns were white, Republican and Protestant. Black people were not a part of my childhood. When I was six years old I fell ill and was sent to stay with a distant cousin, a pioneer woman doctor in Indiana who was a child specialist. She sometimes took me with her when she made her rounds in Marion's "niggertown." I witnessed her matter-of-fact compassion and saw the vibrant dynamics of an African-American community for the first time.

During those years Dad served as a chaplain at a nearby Y.M.C.A. camp. One summer he took me with him and I was befriended by Ellis, a tall, lean, black cook of indeterminate age. We would sit on the back steps of the camp kitchen and talk about things I had never heard of. The "darkies" my mother sometimes talked about were no longer remote beings seen in violent wire photos and featured in *National Geographic* articles about Africa. (As a boy I had leafed through the pages of *National Geographic* for the same reason other curious little boys did.) Ellis introduced me to flesh and blood people who had the same feelings and shared the same needs the rest of us do.

In the early '50s I spoke at a youth assembly in Florida. All the youngsters there were white. Vivian Postell, a young black school teacher who had a beautiful soprano voice, was brought in to help break down the color bar as she sang for our worship services. One day Vivian and I sat under a tree by Lake Griffith and she described her girlhood in Lakeland.

She described a white-robed mob of drunken men lurching down the dirt road in front of her house. Her family stood on the front porch and watched as the men shook their fists, hurled slurs and profanities in their direction, and stumbled on.

She described her little brother tearfully running home and burying his head in her skirts because unthinking white children in a cruel white world, taught their cruelty by older heads, had zeroed in on him hissing, "Nigger! Nigger! Nigger!"

Calmly and sadly she told me those things about her growing up years, things I had no knowledge of and never thought about. And they had all happened because of the color of her skin.

I am back in Florida now and Vivian and I have renewed our friendship. A distinguished black educator, she is retired and has served as Lay Leader of the Lakeland District of the United Methodist Church. She will never be able to fully grasp the contribution she made to my life.

In 1954, when the U.S. Supreme Court handed down its *Brown v. Board of Education of Topeka* decision desegregating public schools, I was in Jacksonville. The combined downtown civic clubs scheduled three luncheon meetings to present differing points of view. An ardent segregationist and perennial candidate for governor (he never made it past the primaries – he was *that* extreme) was asked to present the defiant, "anti" point of view. Florida's Attorney General presented a gradualist's legalese point of view. No one could be found to affirm the *Brown* decision until (probably as an act of desperation) they approached the young associate pastor of the downtown Methodist church. At the appointed hour, with sweaty palms and a trembling voice, I read my statement word for word.

The *Jacksonville Journal* carried a verbatim account of each of the speeches. When mine appeared in print all hell broke loose! Phones rang off the hook. Angry letters and wires came from across the region. Poor Dr. Boyd was besieged by those who wondered why he didn't rein me in. One irate reader tore the entire page out of his newspaper, jammed it into his typewriter and banged out the words: "You ain't fit to be no Methodist preacher. Run this goddam nigger-lover out, out, out quick." That tattered, aging sheet of newsprint is one of my prized possessions.

Twenty years later I took an active part in Senator McGovern's reelection campaign for the U.S. Senate. His opponent was a decorated, disabled former prisoner of the North Vietnamese. I traveled with the senator, made some television spots on his behalf, and wrote media people across the state (unwisely using the letterhead of my episcopal office) urging them, in the light of the grossly unfair caricatures of McGovern that had emerged from the 1972 presidential campaign, to provide equal time for both candidates and to be objective.

Some members from the largest United Methodist church in the state met (I was attending a peace conference in Belgium at the time) and passed a resolution decrying my "participation in political and other secular affairs outside the normal patterns of church behavior." They asked that I "refrain from any further activities of this nature...and give my time...and talents to the ministry of the Gospel."

When Phyllis and I returned from Europe I arranged to go to the church, meet with the people, listen to their concerns, respond to their questions, explain why I had done what I did, and absorb whatever anger and hostility necessary. More than 700 people gathered and we were together for more than two hours. I opened the meeting by reading a statement:

> When I visit Vietnam or represent a church agency at Wounded Knee or appear before a Senate sub-committee or support a particular candidate for public office I do so on the basis of deep ethical and religious conviction, not because of a desire to stray from my Christian vocation. I try not to separate my world into neat compartments, drawing false distinctions between the "secular" and the "sacred."

My church is a free church. The United States of America is a free country. I cherish that freedom and will continue to express it as prayerfully and responsibly as I know how.

I apologized for any discomfort I may have caused them. I confessed I had been wrong in using the church letterhead (25 years earlier I had done the same thing and drew a rebuke from George Smathers for committing the same "sin" – some people never seem to learn). We went forward from there. The next day in a three-column spread, the local newspaper said: "Spirit of Reconciliation Emerges from Meeting of Bishop Armstrong, Methodist Church Critics."

If we choose to become involved in public affairs, dealing with controversial issues, taking unpopular positions, we should anticipate and be willing to live with the consequences. I felt I had no choice but to meet with my critics in Sioux Falls. We have no right to speak the prophet's word (as we understand it) unless we are willing to play fair with those who disagree with us, accepting their right to disagree, attempting to understand their positions, and offering them an open mind and respectful hearing.

As I have already suggested social activism and pastoral concern belong together. Shepherding instincts and caring ministries can be captive to the status quo without the conscientious judgments of the activist. Activism can be little more than arrogant ranting when divorced from grace and common sense. One of the reasons the activism of the '60s fizzled out was because, in too many instances, it lacked civility and soul.

AN ASIDE ABOUT THE EPISCOPACY AND LEADERSHIP

Obviously I did not view the episcopacy as a tame, administrative exercise designed to keep the gears of an institution well oiled and a constituency docile and unchallenged. Yet, a bishop is elected to "bish." There are well-defined administrative duties. The bishop is called upon to preside over meetings including demanding and strenuous sessions of annual conferences. *Roberts Rules of Order* was a stranger to me and I had to learn the governing procedures I would be responsible for. A bishop participates in appointment-making processes each year, working with district superintendents in making pastoral appointments. I had never been a district superintendent and had cared little about the mechanics of appointment-making. When I first met with my cabinets in the Dakotas (most of the superintendents were older than I was) I confessed that I had never attended an annual conference from beginning to end and that I would need to rely on them to do much of my "bishing" for me. They were gracious and tolerant.

I have never been more anxious than before presiding over my first annual conference. There were sleepless nights and conversations with others. I read Dick Blanchard's slim volume *I Remember John* (Bishop John Branscomb was a Florida pastor when I united with the Conference and, in some ways, had been a role model), and did all I could to "get my ducks in a row" (as Dr. Boyd would have said) and psych myself up for the dreaded challenge. I was determined to become a good and effective episcopal leader, and, with the passage of time, I did become more proficient and competent. I presided over my annual conferences with a light touch, never bound by *Roberts,* but blending his "rules of order" with common sense, clear direction and, when possible, with consensus.

I also tried to humanize appointment-making, involving not only the superintendents, but the clergy and their families as well as the congregations, in a tripartite process that was as fair and democratic as circumstances would permit. Too frequently in the United Methodist Church, because of an assortment of pressures, appointment-making becomes an exercise where salaries, seniority, status, "conference morale" and power politics override the needs of persons and churches. The leadership style is more transactional than transformational.

(Let me hasten to add that other polities have their built-in flaws as well.)

Paul Moore, a retired Episcopal bishop, has long exemplified what I think a bishop ought to be and do. He was Dean of the downtown cathedral in Indianapolis when I appeared on the scene in 1958. In 1964 he was elected suffragan of the Diocese of Washington (D.C.). He moved to New York in 1970 as Bishop Coadjutor, and two years later became Bishop of the Diocese of New York. During our time together in Indianapolis we shared much that helped prepare us for the vagaries of episcopal leadership in the latter part of the 20th century. Once a month some of us, ministers, priests and a rabbi, met to encourage and reinforce one another. We saw ministry as a bold witness in an often uncaring and hostile world. In his recent memoirs, *Presences,* Moore described ours as "a strong support group from a variety of theological backgrounds (that) felt totally united in seeking to bring about social justice to Indianapolis. We all had the same problems, but...we did not lose courage."(2)

In an earlier book, *Take A Bishop Like Me,* Bishop Moore detailed his strong convictions concerning the ordination of women and the rights and humanness of homosexuals. On January 6, 1977, an item in the *New York Post* opened with the words, "An avowed lesbian will be among the thirty women entering the Episcopal priesthood this month."(3) The following Monday Bishop Moore ordained Ellen Barrett, a 34-year-old doctoral student at the Graduate Theological Union in Berkeley, into the Episcopal priesthood. A storm of protest followed. One indignant southern layman wrote, "How could you ordain such a filthy, rotten creature?...With a bishop like you, small wonder there is such rottenness, crime and everything terrible in your city!"

With unbecoming presumption I sent a copy of *Take A Bishop Like Me* to every active United Methodist bishop for Christmas in 1980. I received only a couple of acknowledgements, one, a gracious "thank you note" from Bill Cannon who probably disagreed with most of what he read.

Moore described his first meeting with the House of Bishops of the Episcopal Church. "There it was," he said, "a group of huffing, puffing, boring, institutionally protective executives locked into preserving the church at the expense of the world."(4) When I was President of the National Council of Churches I met with and addressed the House of Bishops in Spokane, Washington. They seemed very much like the rest of us. Some were doubtless pompous and self-impressed but wherever "successful" leaders gather, whether corporate executives, university presidents, government officials – or bishops – there is more than enough stultifying ego to go around.

The Council of Bishops I joined in 1968 and left in 1983 was an interesting mix. There were learned educators, "southern gentlemen," pulpit orators, well-organized managers and ecclesiastical mechanics. Most of them were fiercely protective of the institution they had been named to serve. There was a "good ol' boys" network of back-benchers who felt called upon to tell the rest of us what to do. There were fewer of them in '83 than in '68. The Council was becoming more diverse and democratic. There was a time when newcomers were expected to be seen and not heard. That time had passed when I joined the fraternity (it was an all-male tribunal then) and though I was received a bit warily by some, there was openness, encouragement and even a measure of warmth.

I was never awed by the episcopacy. That may go back to my grandfather's sense of betrayal at the hands of Bishop Naphtali Montana (I have no idea what that was all about), or my father's running battle with authority. More immediately, it had to do with the caution and cowardice of southern bishops as they justified a segregated church in the South. Wearing blinders in the presence of injustice they seemed to run for cover whenever controversy threatened their sense of personal well-being or the stability of the status quo institution they sought to protect and preserve. They may have been designated leaders but I was convinced they had lost sight of what the church had been called to be and do in a cruel and unjust society. By the time I

FEET OF CLAY ON SOLID GROUND   45

reached the Council attitudes were changing but there was still far too much rationalization, if not justification, in the face of societal ills.

At the end of my first quadrennium in the Dakotas, not at all certain that I wanted to spend the rest of my days as a bishop, I wrote Bishop Ralph Alton, the Secretary of the Council, asking him how I might "get out." I even met with my College (the bishops of the North Central Jurisdiction) and told them of my restlessness and desire to test other waters. My mood passed, but I suspect some of them never forgave me for even thinking of stepping down from the highest office the church had to offer.

There were some great leaders on our Council. Arthur J. Moore was virtually self-taught. A powerful and eloquent preacher and a missionary statesman, he ordained me. Richard C. Raines, courtly, able and grace-filled, was the one who brought me from Florida to Indiana. And there were James Matthews, a former missionary, a formidable thinker and a dedicated ecumenical leader; James Thomas, a marvelous human being, tall and stately, an educator who inspired his clergy to overreach themselves; and Roy Short, for long years Secretary of the Council, a wise and conscientious administrator. Earlier there had been giants like Francis J. McConnell and G. Bromley Oxnam. Oxnam confronted the House Un-American Activities Committee and in a series of dramatic hearings (chronicled by the *U.S. News and World Report,* and in his own account, *I Protest)* almost single-handedly derailed its witch-hunting proclivities. These men and others like them, joined more recently by women like Leontine Kelly (although no one is quite like Bishop Kelly), were *leaders.* Believe me, all bishops are not leaders. A title does not a leader make.

A spate of books have recently been published on leadership, ranging from the surprising, *The Leadership Wisdom of Jesus,*(5) written by Charles Manz, a professor in the School of Management at the University of Massachusetts, to Stanley Bing's *Crazy Bosses: Spotting Them, Serving Them, Surviving Them.* Bing wrote, "The really great bosses are not great human beings. Gandhi was a terrible boss."(6) He was dead wrong on both counts. Manz regretted that he could not deal with the leadership style of Gandhi in his volume on the revolutionary teachings of Jesus. His arguments would have been strengthened had he done so. James MacGregor Burns in his seminal book, *Leadership,* singled out Gandhi as the finest example of modern leadership, not simply because he wrested power from the hands of the British Empire, but that in so doing he "elevated the hopes and demands of millions of Indians whose lives were enhanced in the process."(7) Jawaharlal Nehru, Gandhi's disciple, became the first Prime Minister of an independent India, as scores of other followers of the "mohatma" became leaders in the new nation. Not long ago Burns cited Gandhi, Martin Luther King, Jr., and Nelson Mandela, as the exemplary leaders of the 20th century.(8) They were not only charismatic; more important, they were transforming leaders.

Twenty-five years ago Burns differentiated between transactional and transforming leaders, a distinction that has shaped the debate on the nature of leadership over the intervening years. We are all too familiar with transactional leaders. Theirs is a tit-for-tat approach to management. They help others achieve coveted goals. The politician exchanges jobs, favors and influence for money and votes; the sales manager exchanges industry recognition and perks for marketing skills and bottom line results; the starlet exchanges the casting couch for a coveted role; the church official exchanges preferred treatment for support on a variety of fronts. This "you-scratch-my-back-and-I'll-scratch-yours" ethic is sadly evident everywhere about us. Transactional leadership tends to be self-promoting, deceptive and manipulative; it caters to the lowest perceived needs and often unworthy aims of followers. Such leaders provide a mutually advantageous exchange of political, psychological and economic assets. Even at its best, however, when based on values like honesty, fairness, promise-keeping and responsibility, transactional leadership is neither enduring nor particularly uplifting.

Transformational leadership, on the other hand, focuses

attention on common goals that have meaning and transcendent value. It looks beyond self-interest to the good of the group. It stimulates the minds of its followers, makes them aware of shared problems and challenges, and creates a vision of new possibilities. It encourages aspiration and fosters moral virtue. Engaging the whole person it often postpones immediate satisfaction for a perceived good. The transformational leader embodies values like kindness, justice, independence and equality; it "elevates" (to use Burns' word) the followers. In the language of faith, it is incarnational.

Burns in his *Leadership* described a collective, collegial, team-building style of leadership. No prima donnas. No solo performers. No lone rangers. Arbitrary hierarchical structures are out of touch with 21st century reality.

Teams cannot be built unless designated leaders develop the capacity to listen and learn from others. Effective leadership is spongelike, gathering data, opinions and impressions. It absorbs and assimilates facts and tries to arrange them in sensible, logical, adaptable and applicable order. I have observed that the longer a bishop, corporate CEO, university president or government official stays in power, the more likely it is that that person grows increasingly insulated and isolated.

The wise leader will be "dissensual" when necessary, according to Burns. Over recent years consensus has become something of an icon among some theorists. M. Scott Peck, a remarkably insightful contemporary guru for millions of Americans, in his book on community-building, *The Different Drum,* says that he has shared in "a thousand or more group decisions" and has yet to see a vote taken.(9) He's either very lucky, a magician or has been spared an exposure to some forms of harsh and demanding reality. Consensus is always desirable but in some instances it is impossible (try on the Middle East or the exploitation of natural resources – and they are not unrelated – for size). Transformational leaders consult with colleagues, listen carefully to other members of their team, gather data from a variety of sources, and then, on rare occasions, must move against the tide – must dissent. If one is charged with the responsibility of leadership one must be willing to run the risks, bear the burdens and pay the price: one must *lead*.

Robert Greenleaf in his *Servant Leadership*(10) has added another essential dimension to our understanding of effective, humanitarian leadership. At a time when scrambling self-centeredness has become standard fare in the church as well as elsewhere, Greenleaf argues that selflessness, a determined respect for the rights and dignity of all persons, a willingness to be "a person for others," is a fundamental requirement for moral leadership.

James MacGregor Burns' transforming concept coupled with Greenleaf's emphasis on servanthood is sorely needed in positions of public and private trust today. *All of the above is directly related to the functions of the episcopacy. In fact, it is applicable to effective leadership, not only in the church, but in every walk of life.*

BACK TO BISHING

The church in the Dakotas taught me much. In many respects it was a genuine Christian community. The vastness of the land, the raw winter climate and the sparseness of the population underscored the need for interdependence. There were very few "high-steeple churches" and no huge salaries so there was very little jockeying for position. Of course the people were human. There were personal rivalries, ideological tensions and generation gaps. Subtle (and not so subtle) forms of sexism were expressed in far too many arenas. Racism, as vicious as anything I had known in the South, victimized Native Americans. (I once met with a group of Citizens' Council ranchers in the Black Hills and heard one of them say, "Hell, Indians don't have souls.") Relationships were abused, vows were violated, crimes were committed (although not on a very grand scale – a bank robber in Aberdeen, sacks of cash in hand, dashed to his car and threw the car in gear only to have the wheels spin on the ice while he waited helplessly to be arrested), and there was regional self-consciousness and defensiveness. But with the passage of time the Dakotas look better and better, exemplifying an openness and warmth often lacking elsewhere.

Another lesson learned. Controversies based on principles do not necessarily weaken the church. Critics of mainline churches argue that involvement in public affairs and the espousal of unpopular causes lead to an exodus of members and income. Inadequate and tepid leadership may do that – the laziness or carelessness of pastors may do that – biblical and theological illiteracy may do that – misplaced priorities and a lack of commitment may do that – but not sincere and energetic involvement tempered by love and pastoral care. Three or four years ago G. Lloyd Rediger's *Clergy Killers*(11) created quite a stir. It was his contention that some lay persons with their unrealistic expectations, unreasonable demands and neurotic needs, "kill" the spirits of their pastoral leaders. While doubtless true in some instances it is equally true that the lethargy, ineptness and sagging morale of some clergy undermine the health of their congregations.

My leadership in the Dakotas was controversial. I was joined by a wonderful corps of dedicated clergy who ran for public offices, were outspoken on troubling issues and deeply involved in community affairs. The United Methodist Church in the Dakotas was considered by most thoughtful observers to be the most relevant religious communion in the region.

My mediating role during the siege of Wounded Knee was seen by some of our people as pro-militant Indian. A few months after the stand-off was resolved Layman's Sunday was observed in some of our churches. In one of them, nestled in a town between the Pine Ridge and the Rosebud reservations, the rancher presiding over the worship service was chaplain of the local American Legion Post. He prayed the offertory prayer saying, "O Lord, we are grateful for this offering taken to meet the needs of others, but don't let any of it get into the bishop's hands." Fortunately, his was an isolated voice.

During my stay in the Dakotas the per-capita giving of the

North Dakota Conference for world missions and benevolent causes led or placed second among the more than 50 annual conferences of our denomination year after year. The South Dakota Conference led Methodism in per-capita giving for higher education. And, at a time when churches across the country were losing members and our region was losing population our two conferences more than held their own. The statistics that reflected the physical and spiritual well-being of the church in the Dakotas from 1968 to 1980 were impressive when viewed in the light of the popular myth that only watered-down, inoffensive expressions of the faith and a witness divorced from worldly concerns are acceptable to most church people.

In 1980 we were transferred to Indiana, one of the largest and most demanding episcopal Areas in the church. My brief stint there was hectically busy and extremely satisfying. My "Impressions" column in the *Hoosier United Methodist* for the New Year's issue of 1981, indicated that I had driven more than 10,000 miles my first four months on the job. I had appeared in each of the state's 20 districts, had preached 67 times, and had participated in more than 40 discussion and feedback groups with lay persons and clusters of ministers and spouses. There had been the customary committee meetings, but I had also spoken at the University of Michigan, Boston University and Illinois Wesleyan. For years some of my critics had said that I was "gone too much." I did have opportunities and responsibilities that took me beyond the boundaries of the regions I served, but I doubt if any bishop in Indiana's history covered more ground, appeared in more churches, preached more sermons, communicated with more people via radio, television and the written word, and made himself more accessible to clergy and laity alike over a three-year period than I did from 1980 to 1983. At the same time I'm certain that some of my predecessors were involved in many more committee, board and cabinet meetings. Leaders should invest themselves in those areas where their primary strengths lie and should learn to delegate responsibilities where others can serve more effectively. Relying upon those with whom I worked and disliking meetings as I did, I delighted in the art of delegating responsibility.

My travels across the country during the years of my general superintendency made me keenly aware of a spiritual hunger that gnawed at the innards of hosts of clergy, and of morale crises among too many of them and their families. In the Dakotas Rueben Job, Norman Shawchuck and Bruce Ough (Job and Ough would later become bishops) developed a pioneering ministry of spiritual formation. Later Shawchuck, working with Conference staff members and lay volunteers, developed similar ministries with me in Indiana. Drawing from the monastic and mystical traditions of Catholicism, from the holiness content of the Wesleyan movement, and turning to Thomas Merton, Henri Nouwen, Kenneth Leech, Anthony Bloom, Richard Foster, Carlo Caretta and renewalists from Trueblood to Kelsey, we held retreats and seminars in local churches, district settings and state parks. We also utilized facilities that would accommodate hundreds of people at Notre Dame University, Oakwood Park and French Lick (known more widely as the home of the Boston Celtic legend, Larry Bird). Shortly after I arrived in Indiana the *United Methodist Reporter* wrote:

> Bishop A. James Armstrong began pushing a pet cause almost as soon as he arrived here last year. That didn't surprise Indiana Area United Methodists. After all, he is the man whom the news media have described as "America's most activist bishop." But what has caught the Hoosiers a bit off guard is the pet cause: spiritual development. (12)

Few if any can realize the feelings of profound guilt I experienced when I resigned in November of 1983. At the center of those feelings were my wife and children, those loved ones immediately involved. But beyond them were the two major challenges that would be left far short of realization. The spiritual formation ministries of Indiana would be aborted, and my presidency of the National Council of Churches of Christ in the U.S.A. would be called to a sudden and humiliating halt.

There are times when I am haunted by the words of my anonymous Jacksonville friend: "You ain't fit to be no... preacher."

CHAPTER IV

"A LEADER MUST BE A BRIDGE"

In my maiden speech as President of the National Council of Churches I made reference to George Thomas' coat-of-arms. The son of a Welsh coal miner and a lay preacher in the British Methodist Church, Thomas rose to become a long-time leader in the House of Commons. He was fond of explaining the significance of the family's Welsh crest. It read, "Bid ben, bid bont," which translated means, "To be a leader one must be a bridge." As the church moves into the 21st century its leadership must seek to span the gaps between itself and other religions, as well as reach out to other humanitarian groups and service organizations. Ecumenism has grown far beyond its unusual beginnings in the revivalism of Dwight L. Moody and the student movement of Sherwood Eddy, John R. Mott and Robert Wilder.

The 20th century was called "the ecumenical century." The International Missionary Council was formed in 1921; "Life and Work" came to birth in Stockholm in 1925; "Faith and Order" in Lausanne in 1927; all converging in Amsterdam in 1948 with the formation of the World Council of Churches.

In this country the Federal Council of Churches was founded in 1908 when 30 denominations ratified its constitution. Joining other cooperative organizations it would become the National Council of Churches of Christ in the U.S.A. The NCC celebrated its 50th anniversary in Cleveland in 1999.

Orthodox communions became members of the WCC and NCC, and the Roman Catholic Church joined in committee work and specific projects with its "Observer" status. However, when Pope John XXIII convened Vatican II he provided the most newsworthy and certainly one of the most significant ecumenical events of the century. Pope John Paul II, though lacking the charisma and bold vision of John XXIII, has continued his church's ecumenical commitments and has initiated overtures befitting Christian leadership in the 21st century, reaching out to both the Muslim and Jewish worlds. It is said that the Pope's trip to Israel in 2000 had three aims: (1) it was a personal spiritual pilgrimage; (2) it was a peacemaking mission in one of the world's most volatile regions; and (3) it constituted a reconciling gesture between the three Abrahamic faiths, Judaism, Christianity and Islam. The Pope used the occasion to apologize for the blind and often cruel anti-Semitism of historic Christianity. A few months earlier, when two Muslim dignitaries had a private audience with the Pope, his Holiness saw that one of them was carrying a Koran and he bowed and kissed it. More recently, old and increasingly feeble, he returned to both Israel and the Arab world. These gestures and symbols were profoundly meaningful in the light of past history. Since September 11, 2001, these forms of bridge-building have become not only highly desirable, but absolutely essential!

While Cardinal Ratzinger's 1999 document, "Dominus Jesus," in which the Prefect of the Congregation for Doctrine and Faith repeated Vatican I's pronouncement that the Roman church is "the *only* Church," and insisted that all other expressions of religious truth are lesser and relative revelations, it is fervently hoped that his document is an aberration and not a reversal of direction.

The World Council of Churches and the NCC have long since entered into significant conversations with both Jewish and Muslim leaders. The landscape of 21st century ecumenism is broadening.

GROWTH IN BRIDGE-BUILDING

I knew nothing of the history or global sweep of ecumenism when I entered the ministry. My early forays into "interdenominational cooperation" were limited and all too typical. There were union Thanksgiving and Lenten services, attendance at ministerial gatherings and occasional joint working projects. When in seminary I hosted a midnight radio call-in program aired on WSB and sponsored by the Atlanta Council of Churches. In Jacksonville I was on an ecumenically sponsored television program. It was broadcast "live" as we discussed the following Sunday's Sunday School lesson. One Saturday morning, with cameras rolling, I finished my work at the chalkboard and turned to join two robust colleagues on a rickety settee. I plopped down, the thing collapsed, and there I was, sprawled out on the floor for all the world to see. Learning how to recover from a pratfall has to be one of life's most valuable lessons.

Far more important than those exercises in interdenominational togetherness were the new friends I was making. Albert Kissling, pastor of Jacksonville's Riverside Presbyterian Church, was tough, courageous, ruggedly handsome and extremely intelligent. He indulged my curiosity, encouraged my community involvement, and stood by my side during the racial struggles of the early '50s. In fact, he joined the Southern Conference Educational Fund shortly after I did and was branded "un-American" by the Florida legislature along with me. Sidney Lefkowitz was the spiritual leader of Jacksonville's Reformed Jewish congregation. A rare intellect, he gave me materials to read and provided a form of rabbinic instruction. I preached from his Jacksonville pulpit and later he would come to Vero Beach and return the favor. James Stewart, a most unsouthern Southern Baptist, made himself available as did Bishop West, once a Methodist who turned high-church Episcopalian. From my relatively parochial, insulated beginnings those were mind-blowing days.

When we moved to Broadway in Indianapolis I deliberately sought out and swam into ecumenical waters. During my first month in the city I approached the executive director of the Church Federation of Greater Indianapolis and the executive head of the Indiana Council of Churches, introduced myself and enlisted in their causes. I met regularly with Fr. Raymond Bosler, editor of the Roman Catholic diocesan paper, Jack Mendelssohn, a Unitarian pastor who had studied with me at the University of Chicago, Rabbi Maurice Davis, Paul Moore of the Episcopal cathedral, and a handful of others, for the early morning gabfests described in the last chapter. For eight years I joined three others, an Episcopal priest, the medical director of the state psychiatric hospital, and a Protestant therapist, on an award-winning TV program called *Insight*, sponsored by the state Mental Health Association and the Indiana Council of Churches. And, because of its proximity and dark, mysterious Byzantine beauty, the Church of St. Joan of Arc became a frequent early morning stop on my way to work. What better place to center one's thoughts and prepare for the day? When my car radio announced the death of President Kennedy (I can remember exactly where I was on Meridian Street) I drove directly to Joan of Arc and slipped into the church with scores of other silent, tearful mourners.

When I left Indianapolis Fr. Bosler wrote in his *Criterion:*

> For ten years (Armstrong) has served as pastor of the capitol city's largest Methodist church...and worked untiringly for ecumenical progress in spiritual and practical matters important to the community. He moved easily among those of all faiths and all conditions and made the social gospel a dynamic, workable force.(1)

During those years I served on the Broadcasting and Film Commission of the National Council of Churches and was a delegate to its last General Assembly before it was restructured.

In 1968, a few weeks before I became a bishop, Phyllis and I went to Uppsala, Sweden, where I served as a delegate to the Fourth Assembly of the World Council of Churches. Senator McGovern was another of the United Methodist delegates, but he was called back to Washington midway through the proceedings by supporters of slain presidential candidate Robert Kennedy. They wanted to launch a mini-campaign to get McGovern nominated.

Martin Luther King, Jr., had been slain just a few weeks before Kennedy's assassination and the shadow of those killings hovered over the Assembly influencing much that happened. The Programme to Combat Racism originated in Uppsala. James Baldwin, brilliant, angry African-American novelist, led groups and circulated among the delegates. D.T. Niles, Barbara Ward, W.A. Visser't Hooft, Martin Niemoller and others spoke forcing me to grow beyond a domesticated view of ecumenicity and introducing me to a more realistic and demanding global view.

Then came the episcopacy and our move to the Dakotas.

In the Dakotas I played a role in the conciliar movement helping restructure both state councils enabling Roman Catholic and Lutheran membership and participation.

When the American Indian Movement seized the village of Wounded Knee on the Pine Ridge Reservation early in 1973 the NCC asked Wesley Hunter, executive director of the South Dakota Association of Christian Churches, and me, to be observers and mediators during what proved to be a 70-day siege. I tracked down John Adams, a uniquely gifted strategist in conflict resolution, in a Chicago airport and asked him to join us. Adams was well acquainted with hot-spots, having represented the United Methodist Church in the Poor People's March, at Kent State and at Jackson State. He had earned the confidence and trust of both federal officials and impatient activists. Living out of a trailer on or near the Reservation (after he had been evicted by the Tribal Council – not to be confused with AIM), his presence proved to be invaluable. Later, in a special ceremony in Washington, D.C., Elliott Richardson,

Assistant Attorney General, said that the work of the NCC on the Pine Ridge Reservation had, without question, averted bloodshed.

My anti-war activities during the '70s widened my circle of ecumenical friends and colleagues. I joined a provocative cast of characters in lobbying efforts, at congressional hearings, on trips abroad, and fasts and prayer vigils, and at a wide assortment of conferences. Among the most memorable were Rabbi Leonard Bearman, Ann Bennett, Robert McAfee and Sydney Brown, the truly heroic Dom Helder Camara of Brazil, Harvey Cox, Episcopal Bishop Bob Dewitt, Father Robert Drinan, the Buddhist Thich Nhat Hanh, Robert Moss, William Thompson and Sister Mary Luke Tobin. As I look back on the '60s and '70s I can't find words to express my sense of gratitude for the wonderment, the sense of meaning, the stimulus and personal fulfillment those days brought. Lasting friendships were made and horizons were stretched beyond belief.

In September 1980, I returned to Indiana as the United Methodist bishop. My offices were in the Interchurch Center of Indianapolis, a concentration of denominational, ecumenical and humanitarian aid offices adjacent to Christian Theological Seminary. During my first stint in Indianapolis I had taught at CTS. The location threw numbers of us together on a daily basis.

Less than two months after arriving on the scene I found myself, joined by Episcopal Bishop Edwin W. Jones, serving as spokesperson for 23 Jewish, Catholic and Protestant religious leaders in a press conference deploring voter apathy, affirming the pluralistic nature of American society, and decrying the belief "that there is only one Jewish or Christian point of view on the complex and troubling issues" of the day. We said:

> We are troubled by what has come to be called "single-issue politics" and by groups that have targeted particular candidates for defeat on a narrow range of issues.

We thought we were in hot water then. Those were days of relative innocence compared to the all-out assault on the First Amendment that is being waged today. With the Religious Right trying to impose its will on party platforms and sycophantic politicians, with widely distributed Christian Coalition voters' guides attempting to tilt elections from county school boards to the U.S. Congress, with an activist Supreme Court calling the historic "wall of separation" between church and state into question, and with President George W. Bush's commitment to school vouchers and "faith-based" welfare programs, church/state separation, one of our nation's most treasured assets and a bulwark of freedom, is under attack as never before in our history.

One of the most interesting and productive ecumenical ventures during my three-year tenure in Indiana took place in the northwest corner of the state. Steel mills had suffered drastic cutbacks and unemployment had soared to more than 25% in Gary and East Chicago. Roman Catholic Bishop Andrew Grutka, the son of an immigrant steel worker, and I, sponsored a Forum that brought industry executives, social workers, academicians, laid-off workers, clergy and the media together. Trying to avert a Youngstown, Ohio, close-down, we joined to develop strategies of recovery. The Forum played a decisive role in the crisis.

In November 1981, I was elected President of the National Council of Churches. It all began inauspiciously. On a brisk Spring day, wearing Levis and a flannel shirt, I was on the roof of our two-bedroom home unclogging drainage pipes and sweeping fallen leaves into oblivion. The phone rang and I climbed down to take a call from Bishop James Ault who was calling on behalf of the NCC's nominating committee. Would I, if nominated, accept the presidency? I stalled. There was my wife and family to consider, and there was my staff. They would be living with the consequences of my decision, enduring the absences and taking up the slack. After treading water for more than a month I said "yes."

The NCC was born in Cleveland in 1950. Thirty-one

years later, in the same hall, I was named its 12th president. In November 1999, we gathered in the same place to celebrate its 50th birthday. Robert Edgar, a Methodist pastor, former congressman and seminary president, became its General Secretary. Andrew Young, a UCC minister, former mayor of Atlanta and ambassador to the UN, became its President. In spite of necessary down-sizing, ever-present financial problems, inevitable tensions, and an acknowledged need to broaden its base to include both evangelicals and Roman Catholics, a new and promising day seemed to be dawning.

In my 1981 acceptance speech I praised the Council for its prophetic vision and record of solid accomplishments, but granted that some of its critics needed to be heeded. "Not the tub-thumpers, racial bigots, 'America-first' ideologues, (and) trigger-happy militarists who (had) seen the Council as their natural foe," but the incisive, well-informed, constructive critics who had said, and rightly so, that the NCC often seemed remote and out of touch, that it sometimes offered simplistic solutions to complex problems, that it tended to scattershot its influence "addressing every conceivable controversial issue instead of being thoughtfully and prayerfully selective." I said that too often we had embraced an adversarial role rather than encouraging constructive dialogue.

The speech was well received. Clare Randall, General Secretary of the Council, and the Council's staff, pledged their wholehearted support. The media was kind. The United Press release referred to my blend of "social activism...strong piety and commitment to spirituality." Bruce Buursma of the *Chicago Tribune* and Kenneth Briggs of the *New York Times,* not known for their gentle treatment of the religious establishment and often critical of trends in the mainline churches, were balanced and hopeful in their treatment of Cleveland. The *Christian Century* said I had "obviously been listening to disenchanted denominational people long enough to pick up some of the needed correctives," and added, "To judge from the bishop's own setting of the agenda, the council may find itself taking the risk of getting in touch with both the Holy Spirit and the grass-roots church."(2) Even the *Indianapolis Star*, long a bitter foe of both the NCC and the WCC, editorialized:

> Bishop Armstrong has the vigor, dedication and reputation which the Council sorely needs at this time...Whatever their church affiliations, all Hoosiers wish (him) well in the challenging days ahead.(3)

Of course there were dissidents. One irate reader wrote the editor of the *Star* expressing shock at the paper's friendly and supportive comments. She wrote:

> (Armstrong) is a far-left social activist, pro-Equal Rights Amendment, pro-Cuba, pro-abortion, pro-terrorist action against pro-West nations of Africa and thinks it's OK to have homosexual ministers in the pulpit...I consider this editorial one more link in the downward course toward total socialization if not communization of our great country.

My schedule had changed. I was not only President of the NCC, but the UMC bishop in Indiana and President of our communion's Commission on Religion and Race. There were 18-hour days, media events and frequent trips abroad – to Korea, the USSR, Austria, Sweden, Geneva, Vancouver and Egypt, as well as every corner of the U.S.A. And there was controversy.

The most dramatic event during my brief tenure as President of the NCC was the unprecedented attack on the Council by *Reader's Digest* and CBS's *60 Minutes* – unprecedented because of the vehicles involved. *Reader's Digest* had a circulation of nearly 18 million, and *60 Minutes* was viewed by 22.9 million households every week. Years later Don Hewitt, the producer of *60 Minutes*, would say that the gravest mistake made during his reign was the *60 Minutes* attack on the NCC and the WCC.

The basic charge leveled against the Council was that the tithes and offerings of faithful church members were being misused, channeled into left-wing, terrorist, Marx-Leninist causes in southern Africa, Southeast Asia and Central America by church officials and staff members. The program was aired on January 23, 1983. Late that night Bruce Buursma of the *Chicago Tribune* called me at my home to apologize for the hatchet job his profession had done on us. William Sloan Coffin, senior minister at Riverside Church in New York City, called and asked if I would like to speak at Riverside the following Sunday to respond to the attack. On Sunday morning, January 30, I presented the "Other Side" from the Riverside pulpit. Needless to say, 23 million households did not hear my reply.

Earlier, having suffered through the crass Morley Safer (of *60 Minutes*) interview in our home, I had sent a 10-page single-spaced pastoral letter to 3000 United Methodist leaders and other church officials in Indiana. I cited articles, commentaries and publications of *Reader's Digest, The Saturday Evening Post,* the Institute of Religion and Democracy (IRD), Paul Harvey, and the American Enterprise Institute. (The AEI's *Ben Wattenberg Report*, aired in the summer of 1982, set the stage for much that followed.) To see the bracketed inset in the *Reader's Digest* article, "Do You Know Where Your Church Offerings Go?" and to see the manner in which Morley Safer deferred to IRD spokespersons Richard Neuhaus and Ed Robb, granting them editorial license, air time and friendliness not accorded the ecumenical leaders on the *60 Minutes* segment, made the IRD's feigned "who me?" innocence and fervent denials that it had played any role in the "documentation" of the program utterly ludicrous. My pastoral letter reviewed three decades of criticism (when a student pastor in Palmetto in 1950 I had preached a sermon responding to Stanley High's ridiculous *Reader's Digest* article, "Methodism's Pink Fringe," in which he claimed that E. Stanley Jones, saintly missionary to India and friend of Gandhi, was a communist sympathizer) and attempted to answer the accumulated broadsides in detail.

Ironically, the attacks were a gift. As President I was privileged to crisscross the country addressing groups and responding to the innumerable questions that had surfaced.

The attacks fostered a public debate that offered the conciliar movement an opportunity to interpret its mission and ministries, educating the "grass-roots church" wherever parish clergy were willing and cooperative, while reevaluating many of its own policies and priorities.

There was an interesting sidelight. William F. Buckley had been after me to appear on his TV show, *Firing Line*, with him. I had ducked. A long-time reader of *National Review* I was well aware of Buckley's intellect, his ideological persuasions and his acerbic tongue. I had watched his program and seen the wily traps the Ivy League Brahman was able to bait so effectively. But, after Morley Safer's deceitful interview I figured anything would be a breeze and off I went to New York to get taped. After all, I would be solely responsible for my end of an hour-long unedited taped conversation. On *60 Minutes* I had been at the mercy of producers, editors and scissors that reduced an hour-and-a-half conversation into a 2-minute snippet – after the jury had already been out and the verdict rendered.

Firing Line went well. When it was finished Buckley leaned over and muttered, "You're damn good," which, coming from him, was about as good as it could get. James M. Wall, editor of the *Christian Century*, wrote:

> Buckley sounded like a 1950's anti-communist... He underestimated his opponent this time. Armstrong is a man who has considerable experience debating the know-nothings in American life who want the world divided into good capitalists and bad communists. The surprise in the debate was Buckley's willingness to sound like anything but the drawing room wit and intellectual he is supposed to be.(4)

Charles L. Allen, conservative pastor of "the world's largest Methodist Church" at the time (First Methodist in Houston had about 11,000 members) wrote and called it "a peak accomplishment in your ministry and one that is a blessing to the church." In the midst of swirling controversy the time with Bill Buckley proved to be sheer fun.

Anticipating the directions in which Robert Edgar and Andrew Young are attempting to take the Council today I did what I could to demonstrate its inclusive loyalties and sympathies. At our first Governing Board meeting in Nashville in 1982, Dr. Foy Valentine, Executive Secretary of the Christian Life Commission of the Southern Baptist Church, preached a rousing sermon on our "peace with justice" theme, and Father Thomas Ambrogi, Executive Director of the Commission on Social Justice of the Roman Catholic Diocese of San Francisco, spoke. Early in 1983, Archbishop John R. Quinn met with the Governing Board and gave a stirring report on the U.S. bishops' pastoral letter on war and peace. I met several times with Archbishop John Roach, president of the U.S. Conference of Bishops, and flew to Chicago to meet with Arthur Gay, President of the National Association of Evangelicals. A visit to Oral Roberts University was on the docket at the time of my resignation.

Equally important was a determined effort to deal with tensions that had developed between the NCC and American Jewish leaders. Many Jews felt that the Council had been unfair in condemning Israeli acts of aggression while overlooking PLO terrorism. They felt that long years of missionary activity in the Arab world had led to a bias against Israel. In August of 1982, I invited 12 national leaders of Jewish organizations to meet with nine persons representing the NCC. We spent more than four hours discussing the Lebanese crisis and a wide range of other topics. Rabbi Alexander Schindler, President of the American Hebrew Congregation, said the meeting was "a sincere attempt on the part of Christians to understand how we feel." Other meetings were held in New York. In St. Louis I addressed a Jewish assembly and spoke both honestly and confessionally about Christianity's debt to our Hebrew forbearers and Christianity's sins against the Jewish people. The late Rabbi Marc Tannenbaum of the American Jewish Committee came to me afterward and we shared a warm and tearful embrace. We had been friends for many years and had testified at congressional hearings together, but this was different.

FEET OF CLAY ON SOLID GROUND 65

The Middle East continues to be a tinder box. James Rudin, now the senior interreligious advisor of the American Jewish Committee, addressed the tensions and continuing impasse in his helpful little book, *Israel for Christians*. He wrote:

> In the quest for a just and lasting peace between Israel and its neighbors, people must not yield to despair, impatience, false optimism or unrealistic pessimism. But Christians and Jews together, armed with facts and faith, with compassion and concern for all the peoples of the region...can work to make a difference.(5)

Rudin and I developed quite a dog-and-pony show and appeared on several panels together.

The United States, in the aftermath of 9/11, and because of the role it played in the creation of the state of Israel, must be a mediating presence in Arab-Israeli talks. Without question there has been Arab-inspired violence, but at whose instigation? The role of the *intifada*, Ariel Sharon's bullying tactics, and the continued Israeli policy of building and expanding settlements in violation of tacit agreements made in Oslo nearly ten years ago (the number of settler houses and flats increased 52% swelling the settler population in the West Bank and Gaza from 115,000 in 1993 to 200,000 in 2000) continue to victimize the Palestinians whose lands were taken from them more than half a century ago. President Carter, President Clinton and now Secretary of State Colin Powell have seized initiatives in encouraging conversation and compromise. Following September 11, both President George W. Bush and Prime Minister Tony Blair called for the creation and recognition of a Palestinian state. Going back to Britain's post-World War I trusteeship of the region, the Balfour Agreement, and the American role in the creation of the state of Israel, their belated call is more than timely.

Churches have a role to play. In my appearances with Rudin I stressed the importance of the traditions Jews and

Christians share, and insisted that we dare not forget the sad history of pogroms and inquisitions, the Holocaust and continuing anti-Semitism (Arabs are Semites too), but justice is justice and we share responsibility for its realization. As Rudin wrote, "Together...we make a difference." And we *can* make a difference, a significant difference, in whatever our spheres of influence may be.

Two other issues emerged during the years of my NCC presidency that grabbed a headline or two: *An Inclusive Language Lectionary* and the application of the Universal Fellowship of Metropolitan Community Churches for membership in the Council.

The lectionary was an earnest effort by competent scholars to make the Scriptures available to a readership that had been turned off by the male images and sexist proclivities that dominate biblical narratives. It was an important contribution in combating the sexism inherent in a traditional understanding of the faith and the customary usage of religious language. Now, 20 years later, the images it reshaped and the verbiage it rephrased are taken for granted in most sensitive and informed circles, but then it was considered revolutionary. When I first read it as a middle-aged male I reacted defensively at points. As with the United Church of Christ's upbeat *New Century Hymnal,* published in 1995, portions of the translation seemed forced and strained. Even so, it addressed a vital need and was another helpful step in eliminating male dominance in the world of religious conceptualization.

The application of the Metropolitan Community Churches divided the Council. On the basis of biblical interpretation and theological conviction different branches of Orthodoxy threatened to withdraw from the Council if the UFMCC was accepted. The homosexual orientation of the Metropolitan churches also prompted opposition from Lutheran and Reformed bodies, and to a lesser extent, from spokespersons representing other mainline denominations. However, there was strong support for UFMCC membership among many conscientious members of most of the communions. Human rights and justice issues were involved. No institution, no person, is without sin. Even the "sin" question was moot. After working with representative leaders from the applying denomination (and those with whom we had been talking for two years were gay and lesbian) it was apparent that their faith was as valid as ours (though usually a bit more conservative) and their love for the church was as strong as ours. I have taught MCC ministerial candidates during my years at Iliff and now at the South Florida Center for Theological Studies. For the most part they have been excellent students and persons of deep faith, who, though often rejected and scarred by parents and a judgmental society, have determined to be of service to humanity through the church. They are no strangers to a theology of the cross.

Following long months of serious discussion and debate, and six months after interacting and worshiping with Fellowship members at our Governing Board meeting in San Francisco, the decisive vote was taken at our Hartford meeting in November, 1983. The outcome, though painful to some, seemed to be a responsible compromise. The membership application was rejected, but the NCC would continue in dialogue and fellowship with the group. They would work with us and we would work with them, but the delicate fabric of the ecumenical council would not be shredded.

In the March 21-28, 2001, issue of the *Christian Century* John Dart wrote of the remarkable growth and "success" of the Universal Fellowship of Metropolitan Community Churches. The only disquieting note was struck when he matter-of-factly reported that "the National Council of Churches denied the MCC both membership and observer status in 1992." In Chapter VII, I will describe my ministry at the First Congregational Church of Winter Park, Florida. Following my retirement from that pulpit in 1999, my wife and I attended many churches. More and more we were drawn to the Joy Metropolitan Community Church of Orlando, a rapidly growing congregation of some 500 souls with an outstanding woman minister. Its worship services are inspiring. Its sense of "family" is exemplary. Its mission outreach ministries, patterned after Glide Memorial United Methodist Church in San Francisco, are second to none in the area. While retaining our membership at the First Congregational Church, we became associate members of Joy in the Spring of 2001. It is ironic – after presiding over a meeting in 1983 that said "no" to the UFMCC, I have, with a profound sense of commitment, said "yes" nearly 20 years later.

The last two major items on the agenda of the NCC prior to my resignation as its President were the lectionary and the FUMCC membership application. I had been closely related to both of them and was determined to see them through as the presiding officer before penning my resignation – but more of that later.

July 24 through August 10, 1983, the Sixth Assembly of the World Council of Churches met in Vancouver. I was there representing both the UMC and the NCC. My role was minor. I hosted a meeting with leaders of the Russian Orthodox Church and other Soviet delegates. I was involved in only one floor debate. A motion endorsing the United Nations position on Afghanistan was before the house. My point was simple. I said, "It is imperative that we vote, not as an extension of the United Nations, but as member bodies of the World Council of Churches whose Lord is Jesus Christ." My words were greeted with a lusty ovation, but my substitute motion was defeated 306 to 270. In that setting Scott Peck's consensus was far beyond our reach.

Participating in one of eight "issue groups" I reacted to continuing assaults on the values and people of the United States. I suggested that American Christians could not serve the present hour by "snarling and turning on (their) own people." "Believe me," I said in response to Dorothy Solle, a German theologian who was teaching in the U.S. at the time, "all is not emptiness in my land...Unrestrained capitalism can and does destroy human values, exploit human beings and subvert God's creative purposes. But," I added, "that is true of every unrestrained earthbound system...Sin is present in every land and among every people." A few days later an editorial in the *Christian Century* said, "In official documents and messages the Assembly appeared to lean more toward the Armstrong approach than toward Solle's."(6)

My ministry, beginning as so many do in Protestantism as a student pastor in a small church in a small town, had developed into something beyond my wildest expectations. I had served a huge metropolitan church, taught in seminaries, written books, and had been featured on national radio and television. I had been elected to serve as a bishop of my church and as an ecumenical leader. As I suggested in my opening words of this volume, "I was riding the crest of a wave."

At the time of my resignation, Charles Austin and Darrell Turner wrote in the *Michigan Christian Advocate:*

> During his 32 years as a United Methodist clergyman, Bishop James Armstrong has followed a career that has blended traditional pastoral care, social activism and on-going attempts to reconcile opposing theological and social views.(7)

In my ministry I had attempted to be a shepherd, a catalyst and a bridge builder. Suddenly that was gone – at least for the moment.

CHAPTER V

"I AM ABSOLUTELY RESPONSIBLE"

No U.S. president has been more himself than Harry Truman – and, unlike many of us, he seemed to know who that self was. After Mr. Truman had returned to Independence from the White House, he and a long-time friend were driving to Jefferson City. They saw a woman attempting to herd "a bunch of hogs" across the road. Truman told his friend to stop the car and the former president helped her get the hogs out of harm's way. When they returned to Independence the friend told a reporter what had happened. The skeptical reporter asked Truman about the incident. Truman in his brusque and simple manner explained that someone had to do it, and anyway, "he'd been a farmer long before he got to be President."(1)

Acquaintances said he had always been the same, whether a farmer, the Captain of Battery D in France during the First World War, a failed haberdasher, a county judge, a U.S. Senator, or the President of the United States. A veteran of Battery D who had known him across the years said, "The thing about Mr. Truman is...he never changed at all." That is highly unlikely. With some people a refusal to change is not a virtue; however, with Truman that sort of predictable consistency was. He was never overly impressed with his place on the world stage. He attributed it to "luck." But, whether at Potsdam or jawing with old friends at a country store he remained much the same. There was little pretense about him. He knew who he was.

Carlyle Marney was right when he said that too many of us confuse our noun-selves with our verb-selves. We become what we do. Our identities are swallowed up in the offices we hold, the honors we accrue and the accomplishments attributed to us. Few things are more important in the lives of "successful" people, or for that matter, in the lives of those who have failed miserably, than to understand that their successes and failures are not the sum total of who they are.

When I began my ministry, and this is true of many of us who feel "called," I had a full-blown messiah complex. I "knew" that God had set me apart for special tasks. With the passage of time I took myself less and less seriously. I was no knight in shining armor, certainly no messiah, I was simply me, and I enjoyed being me; I relished my humanity. My entry into the episcopacy, coming as it did at the end of the '60s, may have been something of an aberration, and I was determined not to let it go to my head. There would be no posturing, no posing, no pulling of rank. I was as flawed and vulnerable as the next person and I would not pretend otherwise. I would be true to myself. Sadly, that self was more Dostoevskian than Christ-like.

Gary Harbaugh in his helpful book, *Pastor As Person,* (2) says that we are our histories, our situations and our choices. In our quest for personal wholeness our choices are of central importance. We are decision-makers. The most fateful, controversial decisions President Truman made while in office were the firing of General Douglas MacArthur and the dropping of the atomic bomb on Hiroshima. He assumed full responsibility for both. The one, he said, was necessary if he was to assert civilian control over the military and avoid a violent show-down with the Communist bloc that would lead to World War III. He claimed that the dropping of the A-bomb, far more debatable, shortened the war with Japan and saved American lives. In each instance he assumed responsibility for what he did. It is no accident that he is most well known for the aphorism, "The buck stops here." Whether we like it or not, that is where it stops for each of us. We are not free *not* to choose. As Dr. Boyd used to say, "Every tub's gotta sit on its own bottom."

Harbaugh is right. We are influenced by our "histories," by our genes and hormones, the time and place of our birth, our family roots and impressionable earliest years. And, we are influenced by our "situations," by where we live, our social and economic status, our physical and emotional health, our relationship to significant others, the schools we attend and jobs we hold, and often by circumstances beyond our control (abuse, rape, the death of a loved one, or by strokes of good fortune). But in the final analysis we are responsible for ourselves. What we do with out histories and how we react to our situations are matters of personal choice. That may sound glib and insensitive, but it is profoundly true. And, like it or not, we live with the consequences of our choices. If the choices are ill-advised the consequences can be costly, even tragic.

When a merchant cheats a customer or a doctor misuses a patient or an attorney exploits a client – or when a minister or priest steps over the line and enters into a clandestine relationship – integrity and credibility are rightly called into question. That is what happened with Pam.

I met Pam shortly after we arrived in Indianapolis in 1958. I had received her into the church, baptized her baby, counseled with her during a bad marriage, a divorce, and a series of later crises, and finally, before leaving Indiana for the Dakotas, had married her to a fine young businessman. She was youthful and vivacious. We had become good friends, exchanging Christmas cards and occasional greetings. When I returned to Indiana in 1980, we saw one another from time to time until, shamefully and inexcusably, I permitted our relationship to become intimate.

In late October, 1983, a small group of us representing the National Council of Churches flew to Egypt to help effect the release of Pope Shinouda III of the Coptic Church. He had been deposed and exiled by President Anwar Sadat. We visited the Pope in the desert monastery where he had been banished, returned to Cairo, and met with Sadat's successor, Hosni Mubarek. There were press conferences, media events and late night idle hours. I used some of those "idle hours" to write Pam and tucked the letter away in my briefcase to be delivered upon our return.

Phyllis met me at the airport on the night of October 28. We drove home and spent a leisurely evening discussing the trip and opening the gifts I had brought her. Later that night she came upon my letter to Pam. She was devastated. She called our oldest daughters and Pam's husband, Jon, and confronted me. There were bitter tears, justifiable outbursts and angry threats. A day or two later our children gathered in our home and confronted me. They talked about my hypocrisy and the casualties I was responsible for. Those endless minutes were the most shattering, heart wrenching moments of time I have ever known.

Only a handful of people were aware of the unfolding drama. I felt it was imperative to continue with "business as usual." I kept my scheduled appointments in Indianapolis, spoke in Louisville, had a cabinet session with my district superintendents in Logansport (ironically, during that session I met with one of our clergy who had been unfaithful to his wife), and returned home to prepare for the upcoming meeting of the Governing Board of the NCC in Hartford, Connecticut.

I knew the course I would have to follow, but I needed to hold myself together through the Hartford meeting. The membership application of the Metropolitan Community Churches would come before us. I had to be in the presiding officer's chair for that one. I had been at the heart of those negotiations from the beginning, knew the actors and was painfully aware of the volatility of the issue. The fateful vote was finally taken and the NCC remained intact. My work with the Council was finished.

I preached my last sermon as a United Methodist bishop from the pulpit of the Matheson Street Church in Providence, Rhode Island, a church that had been served many years before by my friend, then a youthful pastor, Richard Raines. I struggled through the service, preaching on the topic, "Beyond Our Brokenness." Among many other things I said that brokenness "is not only a social and geopolitical phenomenon

– it can be frightfully personal, haunting our most private worlds." I was driven from there to Brockton where I led a workshop. Following my presentations in that setting I went to the pastor's office, locked the door, sat down behind his desk, buried my head in my hands for a time and then wrote out my resignation. For days I had been agonizing over what to say. I had prayed, and read and reread passages of finger-pointing Scripture. The delayed moment of truth had come.

The next morning two colleagues who were fully aware of the circumstances met me at the Indianapolis airport. They had developed a plan of action. One of them would fly to the bishops in San Francisco and hand deliver my resignation to them. I would leave town for several weeks avoiding the glare of publicity. I would go into therapy. I insisted on going to the Menninger Clinic in Topeka, Kansas, and insisted that Phyllis join me there. I was numb. It sounded reasonable. But it was so wrong.

I have never second-guessed my decision to resign. It was called for. But, I should have gone to San Francisco, turned to my episcopal colleagues as trusted friends, and worked through the details of a responsible exit process. As recently as November, 1999, I had breakfast with Bishop James Matthews in Cleveland. We hadn't seen one another for years and there was catching up to do. At one point he said, "It was all wrong. You should have come to us and let us help." Of course he was right. But, I had disgraced myself, humiliated my loved ones and failed my church. My mind was a welter of conflicting emotions. I didn't know what to do and, completely out of character, I let others take over.

In the Introduction I described my trip westward. Phyllis remained in Indianapolis for the time and turned to her children and friends awaiting whatever the morrow would bring. Pam headed for Florida where she and her husband had a condo. I headed west.

The Council of Bishops did the only thing it could do under the circumstances. I have been told of the anguish, the tears shed, a tortuous attempt to be fair and a helpless sense of caring. But, with no other recourse, my resignation was accepted.

I have mentioned my reluctant acceptance of the Council of Bishops' revision of my resignation statement. They changed it to read:

> I have submitted myself to an exhausting and inhuman work schedule and because of this have failed many persons as well as the Gospel.

The focus of my actual text was quite different It read:

> I am absolutely responsible for all that follows.
>
> I have been unfaithful to my wife and family.
>
> I hereby and immediately offer my resignation as a bishop of the United Methodist Church and as President of the National Council of Churches of Christ in the U.S.A.
>
> I am shamed by what I have done to my own loved ones, to another family, to dear and trusting friends, to hundreds of unknown persons who have turned to me for exemplary leadership, to United Methodism and to the Church of Jesus Christ.
>
> ...I have advocated unpopular causes and identified with controversial issues believing I was being faithful to my conscience and the Word of God. I am not here renouncing the message I have preached. I am confessing the sins I have committed.

The statement was unequivocal. The watered-down version confused the matter. USA Today, the Indianapolis News and at least one wire service used the word "burn-out." Burn-out wasn't the issue at all.

The deed was done. I drove west from Indianapolis to St. Louis where I made one final phone call to San Francisco, grabbed a few hours' sleep in a grubby roadside motel, woke up about 2:30 a.m., and hit the road again. I drove to Lexington, Nebraska, where I spent two nights with Ben and Betty Garrison. Ben's father and my dad had been friends serving churches only six miles apart in northern Indiana. He had been "Dickie Ben" in those boyhood days and I had been "Jimmie." We had maintained a friendship across the years. His had been a distinguished ministerial career serving university churches in Bloomington, Indiana, Urbana, Illinois, and Lincoln, Nebraska. (Last year I was talking with an Associate Conference minister in the United Church of Christ who said that as a student at the University of Illinois he had believed little if anything and had given no thought to the church until he found himself exposed to Ben's ministry at the Wesley Foundation. Ben's ministry there had turned the student's life around.)

Garrison had been the prime mover back of my election to the episcopacy, had joined Dr. Boyd and the bishops in the laying-on-of-hands ceremony at my Service of Consecration in Peoria, and had preached my installation sermon in Indianapolis in October, 1980. My "fall" would bring him greater pain than almost anyone apart from my immediate family. His home was a natural haven in the storm.

From Nebraska I drove west to Denver where I lingered with Don and Bonnie Messer for almost a month. Don had been the youthful President of Dakota Wesleyan University and later was called to the presidency of the Iliff School of Theology in Denver. He had been a supportive friend since my Dakota days. I had called him from Hartford as I prepared for my resignation and he had been my line of communication to the Council of Bishops gathered in San Francisco. (The seminary presidents and deans had been meeting simultaneously with the bishops.) It seemed only natural to move toward the Messer home as a place of anonymous refuge. They opened their arms and hearts to me. If I needed to talk they were there to listen; if I needed silence they provided that. Their youngsters, Chris and Kent, indulged my moods and played pool with me. I was made to feel at home with them when their larger family gathered for Thanksgiving dinner. It was a restorative time.

On September 14, 1984, Dr. Messer wrote the "Here I Stand" column for *The United Methodist Reporter*. On behalf of Phyllis and me he called upon the church to manifest "compassion, a spirit of redemption and reconciliation." A few months later he invited me to offer "reflections on (my) resignation" during the Iliff Week of Lectures, the first such invitation to come from a major United Methodist institution after my demise. Less than a year after that, following the untimely death of Ronald Sleeth, I was asked to join Iliff's faculty as Visiting Professor of Preaching. I had been the keynote speaker at Don's inauguration in January, 1982, and was there in January, 2000, participating in another Week of Lectures, when he stepped down as President of the school. He and his family were there for me when I most needed them and I will always be grateful.

In early December, 1983, I left Denver for Topeka and the Menninger Clinic. Phyllis joined me and we spent a week together in their diagnostic, out-patient clinic. Our days were busy with tests, interviews and therapy sessions. We talked with psychiatrists, a fine young family counselor, and spent some treasured time with old Dr. Karl himself.

The Menninger staff was well aware of our situation. My psychiatrist there became a friend. His primary concern was for what he called my "dethronement." How would I adjust to a world far removed from power and prestige? After years of unusual influence could I become an anonymous one among many? Since I had never considered myself "enthroned," the transition was not as traumatic as it might have been, but the radical adjustments and new directions were very real nonetheless.

Given the pressures impinging upon both Phyllis and me, the efforts we made at Menningers' were honest and sincere. In our final session the staff that had worked with us spoke of the likelihood of divorce. In the light of everything that had gone before, haunted by an assortment of memories as we were, incompatible as we seemed, unable to undo the past, we moved toward separation and divorce. I had been unfaithful and there was Pam.

When we left Topeka, Phyllis returned to our home on Anna Maria Island in Florida. I flew back to Indianapolis. Pam had returned there from Ft. Lauderdale. The two of us packed the things that could be crammed into one car and headed south together. In that moment, clouded as our perspective was, it seemed the only way. We returned to her Ft. Lauderdale condo. I rented a tiny apartment and started job hunting. With the help of a retired banker, I was put in touch with Hugh Adams, President of Broward Community College, and George Young, Vice President of Student Affairs. Those three people, the banker and two educators, along with a delightful Spanish-born Freudian psychiatrist, became my "pastors." They accepted me "just as I (was)" and became vital links between my past and my future.

On January 1, I became a consultant for Broward Community College, commissioned to develop a program for some 1500 international students on the three BCC campuses. For five months I consulted with faculty members, talked and counseled with foreign students, read as widely as possible in the field, visited other campuses, and put together recommendations for the development of a long-range program. The recommendations were adopted and "the Armstrong Plan" was put in place.

Following my resignation hundreds and hundreds of letters had been forwarded to me. The words "shocked," "saddened," "bewildered," and "stunned" were repeated over and over again. The letters came from everywhere, from country parishes in Indiana and the Dakotas, to the far reaches of Korea, Uruguay, Ireland, Brazil, Australia, Germany and Switzerland. They were from long-time friends and utter strangers. This correspondence, painful as it was, reminded me that there were hosts of concerned people out there with grateful memories and earnest prayers. Kathy Scales, my former secretary in Indianapolis, and Becky, my Washington-based daughter, provided a noble assist as we painstakingly answered each and every letter.

A newspaper reporter who had been a good friend visited me in my lowly digs. My "kitchen" (a shelf, sink and hot-plate), bathroom and laundry were one, in an entryway off the garage. The other room contained my bed, a work table, a chair, a lamp and a small TV set. (In all likelihood this is what the Menninger psychiatrist meant when he spoke of "dethronement.") As the journalist and I left my quarters to grab a bite to eat he said, "I've heard about repentance and atonement, but this is ridiculous."

In December, 1983, Russell Chandler of the *Los Angeles Times* and President of the Religious Newswriters' Association, wrote an article for the RNA newsletter. In his thoughtful, probing evaluation of the way the media had handled my resignation he asked:

> Is there a double standard for the religious press? that is: "good news" can be dealt with fully while "bad news" needs to be handled obliquely and "softened?"...Is there a double standard for the secular press? Suppose, for example, it had been Jerry Falwell who had resigned as leader of the Moral Majority, chancellor of Liberty Baptist College and pastor of Thomas Road Baptist Church. Would the wire services and the nation's religious reporters have been satisfied with press handouts and statements from Falwell's organizations? Or would they have descended upon Lynchburg, combing every available source and document to dig up the "whole story (or the dirt" depending upon one's view)?(3)

Chandler concluded his article by writing, "Now perhaps I've stimulated some juices." He certainly had! Over the next few weeks reporters descended on Ft. Lauderdale. A stringer from a national news magazine badgered Pam in her condominium. (The secretaries at BCC had been instructed by the administration not to divulge my address and my phone number was unlisted.) What did the reporters want? How far would they go?

I had trusted friends in the press corps and decided to seek their counsel. I called Bruce Buursma of the *Chicago Tribune,* John Long of the *Louisville Courier-Journal,* and Charles Austin of the *New York Times* and Religious News Service. George Cornell of Associated Press got in touch. I was back in the news and felt helpless. The situation was damning enough without being compounded by half-truths, innuendoes and downright lies. One reporter said, "I've been covering you for ten years and you haven't had time to do all that stuff."

In addition to the investigative reporters that converged on the resort city there was the local press. Articles appeared: "Former Bishop is Searching His Soul in Broward," "Former Church Leader Still Plans Career in Ministry," "Ex-Bishop Advises at Broward College" and "Armstrong Searches for Himself at College." It is a sobering exercise to see one's soul bared and probed for all the world to see.

From the beginning Pam and I had difficult, jarring conversations. What was right? What was wrong? We knew. The damage had been done and the hurt was irrevocable, but there was no evading the basic question. Did we have any right to continue on our present course? Pam was married and had young children. Her husband loved her and she loved her husband. I was married. There were grown children. Phyllis and I had shared much over long years. Both Phyllis and Jon filed for divorce, but had we moved beyond the point of no return? What we had done was wrong. The penetrating questions should have been raised much earlier, but they could not be avoided. I kept in touch with Phyllis; Pam kept in touch with Jon. Pam's son from a previous marriage, a pre-med student, visited his mother in Florida and I told him that I wanted to do what I could to return his mother to her home and family.

The hourly, daily struggle was so real. We had not meant to come this far. If we had only foreseen when we ventured those first steps where they would lead. *If only, from my present vantage point, I could sound a persuasive word of caution and judgment to those who are tempted to cross the line.* That which begins as a warm friendship or an innocent flirtation or a welcome diversion can become, with little warning, an irrational and consuming passion. When we lower the bars and permit ourselves to enter into the unconscionable we court disaster.

Finally, decisions were made. In early April Pam headed back toward loved ones in Indiana and I drove across Florida to Anna Maria Island and Phyllis. More was yet to come. Phyllis and Jon had every right to say, "No." But overdue and necessary steps were being taken.

All of this happened nearly 20 years ago. Why reopen the wounds and revisit the sadness and shame of it all? Because in my resignation statement I said, "I seek no cheap grace... Rather, I would have friends and critics alike draw hard lessons from my example." Promiscuity has become a way of life for many as the fabric of a stable and ordered society is being frayed by apologists for moral relativism. While understanding and accepting those who stumble and fall, I dare not encourage by my earlier example their misadventures or help them rationalize their immorality. Let me spell it out one more time – my resignation was in order. As a responsible human being I have no right to shift the blame. I identify with Carl Bernstein who, explaining the failure of his marriage to Nora Ephron, said:

> Let me say, unequivocally, that the breakup of my marriage is a consequence of my actions. Absolutely. There is no question about it...Whatever happened before, in terms of a disintegrating marriage, that's something quite apart.(4)

I remained in Ft. Lauderdale for two more months. My work at the college had to be completed and I had a chastened, grieving, bewildered, remorseful self to put back together.

Holy Week, 1984, will stand out in my mind as long as I draw breath. I determined that Good Friday would be a day apart. I would fast and pray. I developed a list of themes to reflect on: my behavioral tendencies, my pride and ego, the anger and cynicism I was struggling with, my belief system and relationship to the church, the place of personal disciplines in self-development, and the meanings of covenant and wholeness.

I read, reread and immersed myself in the words of Romans, II Samuel 11 and 12, John 8, Luke 6, the second chapter of Mark, the 51st Psalm and the crucifixion passages. It was not light reading and my reporter friend would probably have said that the masochism was continuing unabated, but, for me, it was necessary. How was I to deal with my pain, my grief, my guilt, if I sought to explain away what had happened or simply shrug it off?

I had made my confessions to loved ones, friends and co-workers in the church. But, confession and forgiveness are only points of beginning. How could I make amends for the disillusionment and cynicism my actions had prompted? The soul-searching was both cathartic and productive. I realized there were phone calls I had long delayed. I made them. There were letters I had refused to write. I wrote them. There were specific courses of action I had postponed. How could I relate to Phyllis in a helpful and redemptive manner and recover a sense of direction for my life? Those things would need to follow.

Over the next few weeks there were hurried trips to Phyllis on the west coast of Florida, innumerable phone conversations with our children and friends, job interviews in Florida, New York City and Washington, D.C. I spoke with Pam only twice after she returned to Indianapolis. Both times her husband was there. I have not seen or spoken to her since.

And, there was the winding down of the school year at BCC. I was asked to offer the prayer at the Baccalaureate ceremony, but was told not to do so "in the name of Jesus." Really. Ours is a secular state. The college was a secular institution. In that interfaith/no-faith setting I could be trusted to use my common sense and do the obvious thing. Surely, God wouldn't care.

I donned a borrowed, ill-fitting robe, stood on the fringe of things (feeling very much out of place) and remembered recent graduations at Duke University and the University of Texas where I had been the featured speaker. Maybe "dethronement" wasn't too strong a word after all.

The time came to leave. There were "good-byes" to my new friends, the banker and my delightful landlady, the foreign students, faculty members and officials on the three college campuses. They staged a farewell lunch for me at a Mexican restaurant. I had a final session with Fernando de Elejalde, my psychiatrist friend, although we would stay in touch long after my departure. I had seen de Elejalde on a regular basis and was grateful for his listening ear and thoughtful guidance. We take physicians and surgeons for granted in our culture, but somehow become apologetic or self-conscious when relating our needs to the therapeutic professions. There are still too many people who think that reliance on psychotherapy or psychiatry is a reflection on their ability to function for themselves and govern their own lives. Too bad. It's a sad reflection on our misguided sense of "manliness" and rugged individualism.

At long last I packed my car, gathered my memories together, and headed back toward Indianapolis where I would meet Phyllis. We would go to Washington where I had found employment. We would give our relationship one last try. There were scars that ran deep; wounds that were still open and raw. We could not deny or erase what had gone before. We were still who we were with the same needs, desires, temperaments, limitations and frustrations, and there was a whole new set of reservations. But, time would tell and we *would* try.

CHAPTER VI

"THE CALL HAS NOT BEEN CANCELED"

It is one thing to botch up one's life as the world looks on. It is another thing to adjust to the consequences. No matter what, life does go on. For whatever reason I never doubted my capacity to recover. If I was "absolutely responsible" for my demise I would be equally responsible for my comeback. No one else could do it for me. I had no idea what shape the future would take. There would be obstacles. But, there was enough quiet anger (most of it directed against myself), enough defiance, enough love, faith and commitment, enough adrenaline and yes, enough pride, pumping through my veins to prod me on. And there were dear, dear friends who believed in me, who never wavered – in spite of – and I couldn't let them down.

Having spent nearly 40 years in ministry how would I function as a layman? How would I make a living? Could I build on my years of training and experience or would I have to start from scratch? I had always been aware of the caricature drawn of clergy. We were thought to be naive, out of touch, uninformed, otherworldly do-gooders. I had overcompensated, bending over backward to correct the distorted images of my kind. Consciously or subconsciously I had always seemed apologetic for my profession, my calling. But, I *had* been "called." I had been apologetic for something that should have made me proud. Now, keenly aware of the challenge before me, uncertain about my vocational future, I knew I wanted to harness my energies to something worthwhile, to invest the remaining years of my life in ventures that would not deny the values and idealism of my earlier calling. In a very real sense, I wanted my ministry to continue in one form or another.

A watershed moment came on January 29, 1985. I had been asked to participate in the Iliff Week of Lectures, to reflect on my resignation and report on my activities since stepping down. Some 600 people, most of them clergy, filled the University Park United Methodist Church in Denver. When I rose to speak there was a standing ovation that lasted for what seemed like several minutes. Overcome for the moment I finally spoke my piece, saying, among other things:

> Sometimes we find ourselves involved in indefensible actions. It is important to explain them but not to defend them. We are absolutely responsible for whatever happens to us. To blame others is uncalled for.

I acknowledged my guilt but said that "guilt by itself leads into a blind alley unless we move beyond it to experience forgiveness and self acceptance." I said, "We can't always right the wrongs of the past, but the human spirit can be cleansed and a new course can be set."

I went on to explain my work with Pagán International, a conflict resolution firm in Washington, D.C., and explained my role in the formation of the Center for Dialogue and Development. I referred to my early call to ministry and went on to describe the bridge-building, risk-taking, cause-oriented work I was currently involved in. Suddenly I found myself saying words that had not been scripted, that appeared nowhere in my outline. Almost out of the blue and with deep emotion I said, *"My call has not been canceled!"* There are some things humans can neither give nor take away.

In retrospect my personal life has been richer and fuller since 1983, than it was before. My professional life has continued to be challenging and, for the most part, deeply satisfying. Since 1983, I have been involved in conflict resolution with multinational corporations, have sought to build bridges of understanding between First World and Third World reality, have taught in schools of theology and at the undergraduate level, and for eight years returned to my first love as a parish priest. Now, in retirement, I find myself continuing to teach, write, speak, lead retreats and workshops, serve as a consultant to troubled churches, and be far more available to friends and family than in the past.

As I began life over again it would be important to build on my years of training and experience. Could I do that? The answer was, "Yes."

VOICES FOR JUSTICE AND HUMAN RIGHTS

During my years in the episcopacy United Methodist bishops were expected to visit a "foreign mission field" once every four years. I concentrated on the "southern cone" of South America and returned time and again to Brazil, Argentina, Uruguay and Chile. During the 1970s they were cruel military police states where thousands of people were imprisoned for conscience's sake, were brutally tortured and slain, or simply "disappeared" never to be heard from again. On those visits I divided my time, visiting missionary personnel and Methodist nationals, touching base with denominational institutions and humanitarian aid networks, but at the same time devoting equal attention to ecumenical leaders, the underground opposition, and Roman Catholic activists, especially in Brazil, home of the largest Catholic church in the world, where a distinction was being made between the "church official" and the "church alive." The "church official" was the church of tradition, bureaucracy and the status quo. The "church alive" championed human rights and worked, both overtly and covertly, against the repression and cruelty of the generals' government. Consulting with the Board of Global Ministries of the UMC, the U.S. Catholic Conference, the U.S. State Department, and Latin American colleagues, I became increasingly involved in the struggle for human rights.

I met with influential liberation theologians like José Miguez Bonino and Gustavo Gutierrez, taught with my dear friend Mortimer Arias at Iliff, occasionally interacted with Justo Gonzales, church historian and liberation thinker, and wrestled with the arguments of Michael Novak and other critics of the theology of the oppressed.

There were other valued and strategic encounters. I met with courageous Cardinal Arns in Sao Paulo (one of his first acts when named to the Sao Paulo see was to visit political prisoners) and with Dom Helder Camara, heroic archbishop of Olinda and Recife in northeast Brazil. One of the most impressive human beings I ever met, this frail little man became the voice of Brazil's poor and oppressed. Hated by the military tyrants who ruled his country Dom Helder was nominated three times for the Nobel Peace Prize and was a recipient of the Martin Luther King International Peace Prize.

There was Cardinal Silva Henrique in Santiago, Chile. During the long night of military oppression in Chile he was the one voice for human rights that would not be silenced. He arranged for me to meet socialist President Salvador Allende, and following Allende's brutal murder at the hands of General Pinochet's junta and our CIA, told me he much preferred Allende to Pinochet. "Allende did some necessary things and told the truth," the cardinal said, "whereas Pinochet, who considered himself a better Catholic than me, is a ruthless liar."

In 1972, UNCTAD III and "Christians for Socialism" were meeting simultaneously in Santiago. I attended and participated in both. In 1978, I returned to Santiago to participate in the International Symposium on Human Rights celebrating the 25th anniversary of the UN's Universal Declaration of Human Rights. The contrast between Chile in 1972, under a freely elected constitutional government, and Pinochet's barbaric military police state in 1978, was stark and frightening. Military tanks ringed the plaza outside the cathedral where the closing worship service was held, as scores of people were arrested for demonstrating for human rights.

In 1977, my administrative assistant, Russell Dilley, who had been a missionary in Cuba (and Bolivia) and I, joined Robert McAfee and Sydney Brown, Joy and Davie Napier, and Alan McCoy of the Roman Catholic Church, in Cuba, where we visited government officials, priests and Protestant clergy, hospitals, farms, schools, cigar factories and Defense of the Revolution (CDR) neighborhood clubs. We spent two and a half hours with Fidel Castro (we were scheduled for only 20 minutes, but Castro does get carried away by the sound of his own voice) as he extolled his revolutionary reforms. We asked about freedom of the press, religious practices and political prisoners. He insisted there were none, only "enemies of the revolution." Working with UN offices and encouraged by our State Department I had visited prisoners of conscience at the Libertad Prison in Uruguay and the Villa Devoto in Buenos Aires, but we were not granted that privilege in Cuba.

During the '70s I visited South Korea several times. Although a client-state of the U.S., South Korea was another military dictatorship. I had led a workshop on human rights for the Korean Council of Churches, and in 1982, representing the National Council of Churches, addressed a national assembly in Seoul as the Centennial of Korean-U.S.A. Friendship was celebrated.

During my visits to South Korea I came to know Lee Tai-Young, the first woman attorney in Korea and founder of the Korean Legal Aid Society for Women. She had been imprisoned for her support of democratic reform in her nation, but, though less well known than the Indira Gandhis and Margaret Thatchers of the world, was one of the truly great women of the twentieth century.

I also came to know Kim Dae Jung, now President of South Korea and recipient of the 2000 Nobel Peace Prize for his unprecedented efforts in building bridges to North

Korea that would one day lead to a reunification of the Korean peninsula. How typical of bygone "ugly American" highhanded arrogance was President George W. Bush when he talked down to President Kim, lecturing him about the "dangers" North Korea poses, while restoring it to a "rogue nation" status and, later, making it a part of his "axis of evil." It is remotely possible that Kim Dae Jung knows a good deal more about the Korean mentality and reality than our President, surrounded by hard line military advisors and oil tycoons. President Bush, chastened, humbled and sobered by the terrorist attacks on New York and Washington and the war in Afghanistan, has hopefully turned away from unilateral decision-making and (for the most part) ill-informed opinions.

President Kim was sentenced to death in 1980, by the Korean government for his purported role in the Kwangju student revolt. He had nothing to do with it, but had almost wrested the presidency from General Park in the national election of 1972. His life was spared because of the international community's outrage. The last time I saw him was in Seoul in 1985. I had been asked to deliver a paper at a business conference. He was under house arrest but asked me to come to his home for dinner and a pleasant evening. We talked at length about the future of the two Koreas and of his dream of bringing them together again. After dinner we went to his upstairs workroom where he designed a beautiful calligraphy parchment for me. His name appears on one side of the sheet, mine on the other. Taken from a Korean adage it reads: "To Serve Man Is to Serve Heaven." Framed, it is now a treasured possession that hangs on my study wall.

Why this recital of names, places and events? They were all a part of "my years of training and experience." They helped prepare me for the global dimensions of my conflict management and resolution work, for my "dialogue and development" efforts, and for a much broader teaching ministry than I had known before.

Actually, my post-episcopacy life was jump-started because of my involvement in the Nestlé boycott. In 1979, I had gone to the international headquarters of Nestlé in Vevey, Switzerland, representing two major boards of my church, the Women's Division, and 25 annual conferences, to protest the marketing practices of the huge multinational corporation in Third World countries. I met with the top executives of Nestlé and was offended by their arrogance and defensiveness. They, in turn, had had their fill of people like me traveling half way around the world to tell them how to run their business. As a result of that meeting and the materials I had read I returned from Switzerland convinced that the boycott was justified and so testified before the UMC General Conference in 1980.

Two years brought about surgical changes. Helmut Maucher was named Nestlé's new Chief Executive and Dr. Carl Angst became its new Chief Operating Officer. Nestlé established a Washington office to help resolve the conflict, embraced and set about to implement the UN World Health Organization's marketing code for infant formula products, appointed an independent monitoring committee chaired by former Secretary of State Edmund Muskie, and demonstrated a willingness to meet and talk with critics.

I had made my trip to Vevey, and, following Methodism's General Conference, was appointed to the denomination's nine-person Task Force on Infant Formula. When I became President of the National Council of Churches I resigned from the Task Force and began to work behind the scenes to bring the antagonists together. The boycott was suspended on January 25, 1984, and was formally ended October 4th.

Over the course of time I had developed a close working relationship with Dr. Angst and, although we sat on opposite sides of the negotiating table, a high level of respect had developed between us leading, ironically, to my first job offer after resigning my position with the NCC. Even if I had been so inclined I could not have accepted because the boycott would not be suspended for another two or three months. My acceptance of the position might have been seen as a sell-out by critical observers.

CONFLICT RESOLUTION

In July, 1984, after completing my brief stint at the Broward Community College in Florida, I accepted an interim position with International Business-Government Counselors in Washington, D.C., serving as a consultant. My office was next to that of former Ambassador William Colby. I had last seen Bill Colby in Saigon when a group of us met with him as vigorous opponents of the war in southeast Asia. On January 1, 1985, I became a vice president of Pagán International, an issues-management, conflict-resolution firm in Washington.

Since the days of my visits to Latin America I had envisioned a group of people working together to build bridges between corporate interests in the industrial North and radical social activists in the Third World. For too long they had been talking past one another, demonizing one another, basing many of their angry charges on myths and stereotypical caricatures. I discussed the possibility of a "committee on dialogue and development" with Cardinal Arns in Sao Paulo and Marcos Arruda, an economist with the World Council of Churches, with Emilio Castro, General Secretary of the WCC, David Rockefeller of the Trilateral Commission, J. Irwin Miller, a noted industrialist and former President of the NCC, and many others. Their insights were supportive and helpful.

I also discussed it with Tim Smith of the Interfaith Committee on Corporate Responsibility. He saw such a "committee" as duplicating the efforts of the ICCR and was less than enthusiastic in his response. He was wrong about the duplication of functions. Whereas the ICCR tends to be confrontational (a more than legitimate stance in some instances) it was the stated purpose of the CDD to be a bridge builder.

The "committee" became a "center," never much of one, but a center nonetheless. We had no money and no staff, but we were incorporated and over a brief span of time, we made a bit of a difference.

The Center for Dialogue and Development helped bring World Council of Churches leaders together with the chief executive officers of Nestlé to discuss post-boycott marketing policies and practices in the Third World. It also played a role in bringing WCC executives and Union Carbide officials together following the Bhopal tragedy to discuss humanitarian aid for its victims and multinational corporate policies in India.

Probably the most notable accomplishment in the brief life of the CDD was a meeting Dr. Castro, General Secretary of the WCC, asked me and the Rev. Joan Campbell (then the U.S. staff person for the WCC and more recently General Secretary of the NCC) to set up with a group of top auto executives. On June 11, 1985, we met with Donald Peterson, Chairman of the Board, at Ford's World Headquarters in Dearborn, along with his Vice President and Treasurer, and his Director of International Government Affairs. Later on the same day we met with an equally impressive group of General Motors executive officers. The sessions dealt with the international debt crisis and its paralyzing effect on Third World development. We also discussed the role of U.S. corporations in South Africa and the role of the Sullivan Principles in dismantling *apartheid*.

Those leaders had far more in common than most people would have thought. Ford's John Segan (the Treasurer) was a member of the Advisory Committee of Church World Service. He had just returned from a banking convention in Hong Kong and he and Castro found themselves in complete agreement on the debt crisis. Elmer Johnson, General Motors' Group Executive and General Counsel, was a noted ethicist and a close friend of James Gustafson, the highly respected moral theologian. In a memorandum following our day together I wrote, "One of the chief values of the Detroit/Dearborn experience was the *humanizing* of the leader of the WCC and well-known corporate executives, each to the other." I later learned that those sessions were followed by a series of breakthrough meetings that brought Castro together with a select number of U.S. labor leaders.

My efforts and initiatives with the Center for Dialogue

and Development dovetailed with my Pagán International responsibilities. During my years with Pagán our clients included Union Carbide in the wake of the Bhopal disaster; Campbell Soup due to its policies related to organized labor, collective bargaining and treatment of farm workers in Ohio and southern Michigan; and Royal Dutch Shell and Shell, U.S. A boycott was directed against Shell products because of *apartheid* South Africa's reliance on petroleum products, defined by the United Nations as "weapons of war" in that context. We maintained a continuing tie with Nestlé and the International Nestlé Boycott Committee as we dealt with Nestlé's conformity to the World Health Organization's marketing code.

My time with Pagán was a tightrope-walking act. When they asked me to join them I am sure they hoped I would become another Michael Novak, turning my back on my past and becoming an apologist for big business. Some of my church friends feared I would follow that pathway, too. Had I turned tail I would have deservedly lost credibility and effectiveness. However, I became the in-house gadfly, attempting to interpret and justify the World Council's devastating critique of corporate behavior at Bhopal, identifying with the church's boycott of Campbell products and insisting that there would be no settlement until Campbell was willing to recognize the Farm Labor Organizing Committee and include it, along with the growers, in a collective bargaining process (a contention that proved true), and arguing that companies supplying petroleum products to South Africa would be vulnerable and open to attack by critics for legitimate reasons.

As you can imagine there were spirited discussions on these issues among staff members. My co-workers' walls were spilling over with pictures of Presidents Reagan and Nixon, Jeanne Kirkpatrick and other conservative luminaries. Mine boasted a picture with President Carter, the prize-winning AP wire photo of a screaming Vietnamese girl running down a road away from a napalm attack, and a framed needlepoint that read: "War is not healthy for children and other living things." The fact that I had an occasional lunch with Senator McGovern didn't help matters.

A RETURN TO THE CHURCH

In September 1985, I was asked to become Visiting Professor of Preaching at the Iliff School of Theology in Denver. For eight years, while at Broadway in Indianapolis, I had taught at Christian Theological Seminary. I loved teaching and if I moved to Denver I could maintain my connection with Pagán in Washington (I commuted between Washington and Denver every other week for two years) while devoting my primary attention to helping give shape to a new generation of clergy. The opportunity was a godsend. The classroom had always been stimulating and rewarding and this move would signal a return to the life of the church. I was more than ready. Phyllis and I had made an earnest effort, but our attempts at reconciliation had been futile. She would leave Washington for her home in Florida. I once again drove west toward Denver.

The years at Iliff were restorative. Of course, there were the negatives – faculty egos and insecurities, committee meetings without end, the temptation to turn the seminary into a professional school of religion while de-emphasizing ministry in and through the local church, and the pettiness that is part and parcel of the human condition no matter where one finds oneself. But, far more important were the privilege of interacting with students, the gifts of new friendships, the generosity of colleagues, the stimulating disciplines of the academy, a return to the life of the church, and, not least, the rugged beauty of the Rockies. I taught the basic courses on preaching as well as "social ministries," served as a student advisor, directed field work studies, and, with Dana Wilbanks, the Christian ethicist, developed a course on, "Corporate Ethics and Third World Reality," a course I took across the campus to the University of Denver's School of Business. That particular course, drawing on my experiences in Latin America and Asia, and on my time with Pagán International, refined and updated with the passage of time, is now offered at the Hamilton Holt School of Rollins College in Winter Park, Florida. The course has been renamed "Big Companies in Little Countries," a far sexier title.

After nearly twenty years of globe-trotting, administering the affairs of the church, addressing a wide range of issues, and functioning with a measure of success in the secular world, life at Iliff was like returning to the parish ministry. I related to the same people day after day, counseled with both students and faculty and became a part of their lives. They were in and out of my apartment, and I was with them in their dorms and homes. I became their confidant and friend.

A PERSONAL NOTE

One of my students was Carol Sue Harper, a mother of young teenagers, who had come from west Ohio. She turned westward because of her love for the mountains, her love of skiing and back-packing, and because there was a seminary that could meet her needs. Of course, there were other United Methodist seminaries (two in Ohio), but there was only one mountain range called "Rocky." I was named her advisor. Later she became my part-time secretary as I maintained my Washington connection with Pagán. Our relationship ripened, became more serious, and a year after her graduation, in December of 1989, Sue and I were married. Sue's daughters, Allison and Eve, "presented" her for marriage in the ornate Iliff chapel. Her brother, Morgan, a hospital chaplain in West Virginia, was there. My daughters, Terri and Leslye, were there, as were students, faculty members and a few close friends. In a profoundly meaningful way the ceremony symbolized a new beginning.

Allison and Eve became "mine." They were wonderfully alive and full of mischief. They loved their mother, were fiercely loyal to one another, and embraced me (after a few initial fits and starts) as their very own. I was older and wiser now. I had learned costly lessons in my first marriage and made myself available to them. We played, laughed, worked, studied, and traveled together. I became an integral part of their lives as they continued to grow. I never tried to take the place of their father who, during our Denver years, lived nearby, but ours became a unique relationship. When she turned 18, Allison, the oldest, changed her name to "Armstrong." Eve calls me "Pops" or "Dad Two," or "Jimmie" (I allow very few people to call me "Jimmie"). The two girls graduated from high school and went on to earn their undergraduate degrees at Colorado State, Allison in Molecular Biology and Eve in Sports Science. Alli continued with graduate studies at the University of Washington and is now a Research Assistant with a pharmaceutical firm in Seattle. Eve has fulfilled an ambition she had harbored since her early teens and is on the management team of Nike Team Sports at their international headquarters in Beaverton, Oregon. Since I now teach a course on "big companies in little countries," and since Nike is a prime example of one of those companies, we have some animated conversations about child labor, "sweat shops" and factory conditions in Latin America and southern Asia.

Let me get ahead of my story for a moment. Sue and I came to Florida in July of 1991. The girls were in school in Colorado but spent their summers and vacations with us. Although rooted in the West, Winter Park became their other home.

After graduating from Iliff Sue chose not to be ordained. In Denver she became the first Executive Director of Mothers Against Drunk Driving. When we came to Florida, cause-oriented and determined to harness her energies to human well-being, she became Executive Director of the Florida Coalition Against Domestic Violence. Later, for five years, she served as the senior executive of Planned Parenthood of Greater Orlando. I identified with and took tremendous pride in her work, even as I do now as she directs the activities of the American Civil Liberties Union in Colorado. (She has returned to her beloved Rocky Mountains.)

Our life together was peaceful and good, fun-filled and more than compatible. We shared so much – our wary and sometimes skeptical love for the church, our devotion to family, our love for the sun, our politics and social idealism, and our humor – lots of humor. Our marriage, though now over, was a wonderfully satisfying season of my life.

In the summer of 1997, while on a sabbatical in the Colorado mountains, Sue was diagnosed with lymphoma. She returned to Florida, had radical surgery (a nine-pound spleen was removed), and underwent five horrendous months of chemotherapy. Medical science, the prayers of hundreds of people across the country, and her own indomitable spirit pulled her through. She is now in remission. In many respects her illness brought us closer together. However, the illness caused Sue to focus on her future in new ways. We had come upon an article in the *New York Times* by Elaine Louie, "After Cancer A Whole New Attitude,"(1) that proved to be a portent of things to come. After citing a number of instances the author wrote, "Cancer survivors often go through radical life changes. They switch jobs, spouses and friends."

After vacationing in the Rockies during the summer of 1998, Sue accepted a position in Denver. She moved west in August. I remained in Winter Park to close out my ministry at the First Congregational Church. Although we had talked about living separately much of the time, and of my retaining living quarters in Florida so that I could continue teaching, in January she wrote that she had filed for divorce. She would always love me and treasure our time together, she said, but she needed to be able to function as "a single woman" in her new home. Her happiness and well-being were involved and it became a mutual decision. I didn't share the news with the church because I didn't want a cloud to hover over my approaching retirement. In early April, 1999, Sue and the girls came back for my retirement ceremonies. It was a difficult time, especially when Brenda White, a dear African-American friend, sang, "May the good Lord bless and keep you..." but we moved through the event grateful for the years we had shared in the Winter Park church and community. While they were here the girls and I had loving and mutually supportive conversations. Sue and I spent necessary time talking about our futures and I told her

I would be seeing other persons and would be moving ahead. Her parents and brother, Morgan, remain treasured friends. The girls and I will always be bound by the strongest of bonds. And, I will always cherish my time with Sue, but, I was 74, my remaining days were numbered and time really doesn't wait for anyone.

❦

Now, back to the Spring of 1991.

My initial Iliff contract was for one year only, then there was a second contract for two years, then a third one for three. It was about to expire and the Rocky Mountain Conference of the UMC asked me to consider going to the University of Colorado in Boulder where I would be the Methodist chaplain. The church, parsonage and student center were across from the huge all-purpose stadium where Bill McCartney's football team had just won the national championship. McCartney was well known in Colorado for espousing right-wing causes. A self-confessed "born-again Christian" he spoke out against proposed state legislation designed to guarantee homosexuals their civil rights. He was an ardent "right-to-lifer," appearing at rallies all over the region opposing abortion. His primary claim to fame was as the founder and dominant voice of the Promise Keepers movement. Those who knew me best envisioned, with a dash of wry humor, what they felt would be an inevitable face-off between McCartney and myself. It was not to be.

In coming to Denver I had returned to the life of the church. I had held preaching missions, led Pastors' Schools, and become active in the Rocky Mountain Conference of our church. However, my first and primary task was to teach aspiring pastors "how to preach." Soon after I left Iliff, *An Intellectual History of the Iliff School of Theology – A Centennial Tribute 1892-1992,* was published. One chapter was devoted to "Homiletics and Preaching Over Four Decades." The writer who described my teaching at Iliff employed an extravagant amount of purple rhetoric. He said:

(Armstrong's) courses, like the sermons he preaches, were as relevant as the morning paper and as deep as the ancient truths on which they were grounded. They danced with vitality, sang with hope, sounded with compassion and rang with the good news of God's redeeming love. James Armstrong, as professor of preaching, helped shape in a powerful way those who through their preaching would help shape our communities of faith and our world...After teaching at Iliff for six years James Armstrong left Denver in July, 1991, to become Minister of the First Congregational Church (United Church of Christ) of Winter Park, Florida.(2)

"...left Denver...to become minister of the First Congregational Church of Winter Park." *The call had not been cancelled!*

CHAPTER VII

"NEW ALPHAS"

My retirement from the pastoral ministry came after eight wonderful years at the First Congregational Church of Winter Park. At the time of my retirement Dr. Martha Hopkins, Moderator of the church, wrote "An Open Letter to Dr. Armstrong" that appeared in the Carillon, our church's monthly newsletter.(1) It read:

> Dear Jim:
> It seems like only yesterday that you and Sue stood before a group of discouraged, confused and somewhat contentious folks promising to love them and encouraging them to open hearts, minds and souls to you, your ministry and God (not in that order). Then again, those days seem remarkably distant. To look at us now, eight years later, we've become part of a spiritually healthy, forward-looking, thriving congregation that not only tolerates, but celebrates diversity of thought among its members. You offered us hope, guidance, support, leadership and love.
> You gave us new life.
> How did you do it? That will forever remain a mystery. But we're afraid, dear Jim, that you've left some clues lying around. First of all there were your sermons...You were able to hold us spellbound while telling us the hard things about Christianity we didn't

want to hear. You helped us see the relevance of the scriptures in our daily lives, challenged us to take action against injustice, and forever reminded us of God's grace and redeeming love. We laughed with you. We cried with you. We even got angry a time or two. But we never lost sight of the importance of living the Christian life. Every congregation needs an effective teacher and preacher. Thank you!

The second clue can be found in the words and emotions of those whose lives you touched while they were suffering pain, illness or loss of a loved one. Compassion, love, comfort, understanding, listening...you seem to have given each of these words new definition. Every congregation needs a pastor. Bless you.

We found the third clue in the church building itself. Who would have thought that we could raise over $1,000,000 in a capital campaign after only two years of your ministry? Was this a sign that we were already healed, or was this a part of the healing process? We suppose we'll never truly know the answers to this question, but the success of the campaign speaks volumes about your ability to help us work together for the good of the entire community, and to recognize and appreciate the special talents each one of us has to offer. Every congregation needs an effective leader. Thank you!

Another clue can be found in and around the church whenever a board or committee is meeting; the energy emanating from these boards and committees as they deal with issues in the present and plan for those of the future is second to none! Members of the congregation who would not otherwise work or play together are drawn to the church through a common interest, working together to enrich the lives of all members of the congregation. Every church needs an effective facilitator. Thank you!

Clue number five is the quiet hum of the administrative engine as the staff works effectively toward a common sense of ministry. Your constant reminders to the staff team that they are called to serve God and the congregation has kept everyone working together while giving a sense of purpose to each individual's professional growth and development. We have been spoiled by the high standards of quality you have nurtured. Every congregation needs an inspiring administrator. Thank you!

There are many other clues lurking about, but the last one we want to share with you is the effect your ministry has had on our relationship with the greater community. By example, you have encouraged us to look beyond ourselves as we seek to discover the breadth of God's love. As members of the congregation have followed you to Bridgebuilders, Habitat for Humanity, the Coalition for the Homeless, the Family Service Center, the Florida Council of Churches and the Winter Park Interfaith Fellowship we have been enriched beyond measure. It seems the more we work and play with others, the stronger we become ourselves. Every congregation needs a leader to help them see beyond their own microworlds. Bless you!

So, the strength of our congregation is not such a mystery after all. You helped us appreciate ourselves while encouraging us to appreciate others. You taught us how to love and be loved.

Diverse though we may be, we are one in Christ. By giving so generously of yourself you have given us the most precious gift of all – new life.

I have received honorary degrees, been published and been elected to high office, but no tribute has meant more to me. Much credit for the ministries Marty enumerated belonged to Jana Norman-Richardson, my associate and co-pastor for nearly six years, whose remarkable creativity, team-building skills and attention to detail made their own unique contribution to our shared ministry. Jana wrote in the same issue of the *Carillon,* "Jim is defined and driven by an abiding commitment to love God with heart, soul and mind and to love neighbor as self. This commitment pushed him beyond his own self-interest, past the unnecessary clutter, straight into what is most loving and transformative." Marty's and Jana's words, more than generous and surely exaggerated, summarized what I wanted my ministry to be. That ministry began in New Port Richey in a small frame church; its pastoral dimension ended in Winter Park in a lovely, New England-style edifice. Both were local congregations. That's the way it should have been. The local church *must* be seen as the core unit of God's earthly realm.

I referred to my years at Broadway in Indianapolis as "glory days" and said that that congregation represented the promise and relative actualization of a true community of faith. To a lesser extent, because of the church's location in an affluent community, and the fact that it was the '90s and not the '60s, and I was in my late 60s and not my 30s and early 40s, Winter Park's First Congregational Church also had its own special aura.

The call to Winter Park was unusual in many respects. Charles Burns, the Conference Minister of the United Church of Christ in Florida, had seen in the *Christian Century* that I was about to leave Iliff. He called and asked if I would consider serving a UCC congregation. I was open to the possibility but I had been asked to go to the University of Colorado. The normal search process in congregational polity takes long months. I didn't have "long months." I would have to give the Rocky Mountain Conference of the UMC an answer by June 1, and it was already May. Sue and I flew back to meet with the necessary groups. They were guarded but friendly. I wasn't Congregational, I was "old" (and getting older), I had been divorced, and my present wife was suspiciously young. The exchanges were candid and honest. Sue and I flew back to Denver knowing that we were about to change the direction of our lives.

The call was unusual not simply because of the change in denominations, but because of the circumstances surrounding my predecessor's departure. He had served the church only 18 months, there had been difficulties, he was pressured into resigning, and the manner of his exit left much to be desired. The church was sharply, one observer said "pathologically," divided, with angry, anonymous letters flying back and forth across the parish. I had been made fully aware of the divisions and knew what to expect. Matters were compounded when a lead article in the *Orlando Sentinel* on my predecessor's final Sunday in the Winter Park pulpit announced my coming and identified me as a former United Methodist bishop who had left the episcopacy because of "an alleged extramarital affair." My "call" had not been announced to the congregation and the breaking news proved to be a bit much. Another trip back from Denver was necessitated. There was a heated, standing-room-only congregational meeting with withering questions and a host of friendly, supportive comments. My responses were as candid as I could make them. Understandably, not everyone was pleased, but a remarkable sense of unity emerged from a very difficult situation. No one had been misled. There was no duplicity involved. On Sunday, July 14, 1991, my ministry in Winter Park began as I preached on the topic, "Why Are We Here?"

There was still acrimony in the air and the first eighteen months of my ministry were devoted, in large part, to offering myself to the people and shepherding the flock. There were the teaching and preaching, routine pastoral duties and counseling, hospital and nursing home visits, weddings and funerals, administrative and fiscal responsibilities – things James Glasse used to call "paying the rent." But, more important than anything else, was the healing process. It had to be woven into every phase of the congregation's life.

In my final annual report to the Winter Park congregation I recapped a handful of statistics. From 1991 to 1999 we had received 623 members into the church with a net gain of almost exactly 200, from 751 to 950. That may not seem very impressive in a region of mega-churches and Southern Baptist, United Methodist and Pentecostal behemoths, but it was notable for a downtown church in a community with little population change over two decades because of zoning laws, building codes and an overriding pride in the beauty and culture of the status quo. The income of the church rose from $214,000 in 1991, to $605,000 in 1999. A $1 million capital fund drive was conducted, and a classic Aeolian-Skinner organ was retooled and modernized.

At the biennial meeting of the Florida Conference of the United Church of Christ, held in the Fall of 2000, our church was given a plaque offering "grateful acknowledgment" for being "first in the total dollar increase in contributions to the basic support of Our Church's Wider Mission" from 1995-1999. Friends from former incarnations will think old Jim has really "lost it," writing about such mundane things as membership rolls and money, but every stat cited represented someone's selfhood and commitment, and such things are important if the local church is a significant part in God's scheme of things.

The village of Winter Park came into being in the early 1880s. It claimed its name, "Winter Park," in 1881. On October 12, 1882, the Rev. S. B. Andrews, a Congregational minister from New England, held its first religious services "in the Town Hall above Ergood's store." The church was formally organized in 1884. A town historian described it: "Planks resting on nail kegs were the first pews; a pine table and kitchen chair served as the pulpit; cheese cloth in the windows kept out the insects but not the chill." Dr. Edward Payson Hooker, a direct descendant of one of the founders of Connecticut, became the first pastor. A year later the church was instrumental in the founding of Rollins College, now one of the outstanding liberal arts colleges in the southeast, and Dr. Hooker became its first President. Over recent years the first Sunday of each November has been observed as Founders' Day, and two worship services have been held, one at First Congregational and one in beautiful Knowles Chapel on the Rollins campus, with the college President, the Dean of the Chapel, and clergy from the church, participating. It was only natural that I became an adjunct faculty member shortly after our arrival and continue in that capacity to this day.

One of the most satisfying aspects of my Winter Park ministry was the formation of Bridgebuilders, an interfaith, interracial community organization. Shortly after she became Moderator of the church, Judge Alice White and I had breakfast. She asked me what I hoped to accomplish during my ministry in Winter Park. My responses were mundane and predictable. I wanted to bring it both stability and excitement so that, when the time came for me to leave, anyone in the country would consider it a privilege to come to our pulpit. It was a stock answer and she obviously wanted something more substantial. "Yes, Jim," she said, "but what of *real significance* do you want to see happen?" As we talked further she argued that as an affluent and influential congregation we would either relate to the west side of our town in new and redemptive ways or we could lose our collective soul. She was right.

About 4000 African-Americans live on the west side of Winter Park. A part of the history of Winter Park from its beginnings, they were politically disenfranchised during the early years of the 20th century and have been largely ignored and abjectly neglected by the city fathers (one or two "mothers" have emerged over recent years). Following our breakfast conversation a "blue ribbon" committee was named to give specific consideration to our mission on the west side. The Mayor, a School Board official, a land developer, representatives of social service agencies, a retired minister with extensive experience in urban ministries, and a few other concerned members as well as a couple of eager young people, were appointed to serve.

Hearings were held and some of them were wild. Angry and often conflicting voices were heard. We met with a developer who was gobbling up choice properties on the west side for commercial development and what appeared to be mercenary gain. We were determined not to provide "answers" from outside the community, but to simply listen and wait for a sense of direction.

Lake Island Park, wedged between black residents and commercial developments on a major thoroughfare, was redesigned and refurbished by the city. Our Task Force was asked to help celebrate its reopening and plan a dedication ceremony. Rather than plan *for* the west side we set up an organization with co-chairs, one white and one African-American, for each of the working committees. Working with the City Commission and park officials we planned and "manned" (most of the co-chairs were women) a day-long celebration for Saturday, October 19, 1996, and assumed responsibility for the rededication ceremonies the following afternoon. Bishop Cornelius Henderson, the first African-American episcopal leader to come to the Florida Conference of the UMC, was the featured speaker. The highlight of the occasion was the ribbon-cutting ceremony dedicating Unity Bridge. The mayor and the bishop wielded the scissors. Rick Mildner, one of the co-chairs of the event and a member of First Congregational, spoke. He said, "You can't build and keep and grow a bridge called Unity without the effort of the whole community. That's hard work. But it's worth it. Unity is a bridge worth building." Out of that initial cooperative effort Bridgebuilders came into being.

Bridgebuilders, ably assisted by civic clubs, has sponsored an Easter sunrise service each year as community choirs and salt-and-pepper children's groups sing. Catholic and Protestant clergy preside as several hundred people gather to worship.

Stressing the interdependence of neighborhood organizations Bridgebuilders has tried to be an umbrella, working with and coordinating the affairs of other community interests. In 2000, it formed an independent 501(c)(3) entity, the Winter Park Neighborhood Development Corporation, that encourages and facilitates housing and development activities. Committed to empowering residents of the west side it has a political action committee. Volunteers engage in neighborhood cleanup and landscaping projects. Meeting on a monthly basis at the Mt. Moriah Baptist Church it has involved citizens from both sides of the tracks (quite literally white Winter Park is on the east side of railroad tracks that split the city down the middle; black Winter Park is on the west side) as it tries, in its own words, to "ensure that all persons living in Winter Park work together to create racial harmony, safe and secure neighborhoods, and make a sensitive and informed response to the needs of the residents." Racism continues to thrive in the U.S. It must be dealt with at the grass roots of our common life.

Race, peace and the environment were clearly-defined issues that loomed large in the '60s. They remain with us today and have been clearly joined by issues related to women's rights and human sexuality.

Without politicizing the issue, First Congregational welcomed gays and lesbians into its fold including more than one former United Methodist who no longer felt free to live under the constraints of the "official position" of that denomination. I led workshops for Parents and Friends of Lesbians and Gays (PFLAG), met with its national board, and took my place at press conferences condemning sexual bias. While retaining our membership in the United Church of Christ my wife and I, as I indicated earlier, have become associate members of the Joy Metropolitan Community Church.

The ordination of gays and same-sex unions are prompting stormy debates in many church bodies, yet, on the basis the counseling I have done, countless conversations I have had, and in the light of authoritative books I have read, I am convinced that the orientation of most gays and lesbians is natural and therefore God-given. It is not something they have chosen, *it is who they are.* And, as some are fond of saying, "God doesn't make mistakes."

Two of my closest male friends were gay and, interestingly enough, I had no idea either of them was a homosexual until we had worked together long months. Both were well-educated, highly intelligent and singularly gifted. One remained closeted his entire life while holding sensitive positions and fearing exposure. The other one married (his wife was fully aware of his struggle), fathered a child then sadly, reluctantly, accepted who he was and left the marriage. He retained a close relationship with his former wife and growing son.

He died a few years ago. His funeral was held in Washington's Church of the Epiphany where he had been a vestryman. The church was filled with friends and former co-workers. His son, about to graduate from college and be married, sat with his father's partner of fourteen years during the service. When asked to speak, his son paid tribute to his father's integrity, courage, caring nature and self-giving love. Finally he said, "You ask me what legacy my father left behind? There is much, much more, but *here I stand.*"

Most of us don't identify with an issue unless we personalize it. My first namesake and godson was James Armstrong McIntyre, born August 8, 1960. Known as "Jimmy Mack" he became music director of Boston radio station WBCN-FM while still in his teens. He was gay, contracted AIDS and died at the age of 25. An article in the *Sudbury Town Crier* chronicled the last year of his life. It said he "devoted precious time and energy to educating people about AIDS." He worked with the Boston AIDS Action Committee, the National Association of People With AIDS, and the national AIDS Action Committee. He spoke to business groups, student groups, clergy and health providers, often speaking three or four nights a week.

At his funeral, just before 25 balloons were released into the cloudless Boston sky, a woman stood and said, "Life is short but sometimes very wide. I think Jimmy's life was very wide." Jimmy's picture hangs on my workroom wall.

On August 10, 1987, *Newsweek* published a special edition on, "The Face of AIDS." It featured a gallery of 302 men, women and children who had succumbed to the epidemic over the prior 12 months. One of the names and faces was that of United Methodist Bishop Finis Crutchfield who had died in May of that year. Crutchfield was a social and religious conservative. When I was still in the Dakotas I received an angry call from a young church staff member who was gay. He said he and some of his co-workers were going to "out" the bishop if he continued to speak out against the things they believed in. Would I "warn" him? I had no knowledge of the bishop's sexual orientation, but I did call and told him of the implicit blackmail. I assured him I had no interest in his proclivities but was calling as a concerned colleague and friend. Before I hung up I said, "It's possible there are times when you may feel very much alone on the Council. If you ever need a friend or pastor I am here for you."

On the Council of Bishops Crutchfield and I seldom agreed and often found ourselves on opposite sides of debates, but that phone conversation sealed a warm friendship. When I resigned in 1983, no bishop showed more compassion. He called and said, "I'll give you any church in Texas" – which wasn't exactly what I had in mind at the time.

During the bishop's final illness I was with Pagán International in D.C. One of our clients was Shell, U.S., headquartered in Houston. My friend was in the Methodist Hospital there. Combining business with an opportunity to see Finis I flew into Houston, drove to the hospital and spent a precious few minutes with him and his devoted wife. We prayed together, committing our remaining days and endless futures to God. *When we humanize an issue it tends to take on a radically different meaning for us.*

Abortion along with homosexuality is a hot-button issue in the church and nation. My wife, Sue, was Executive Director of Planned Parenthood of Greater Orlando for several years and I was a member of her Advisory Board. Although no abortions were performed in her clinic it was subject to pickets and demonstrations. In central Florida, home of Disney's Gay Pride Day and one of the buckles on the region's Bible belt, confrontation was a way of life.

In March, 1993, I spoke "words of hope" at a memorial service for Dr. David Gunn, a physician who performed abortions at a clinic in Pensacola and who was gunned down by a religious fanatic. (My message was reprinted in *Prayerfully Pro-Choice,* published by the Religious Coalition for Reproductive Choice.) I spoke at a memorial service for Dr. John Britton and James B. Barrett, also killed in Pensacola outside an abortion clinic just 18 months later. Britton once said, "Being shot by a madman is always a risk." It happened on a July day in 1994 when a madman opened fire on him and the man accompanying him to the clinic.

Although, as I indicated earlier, I seldom preached on single, controversial issues, on the Sunday following Easter in 1993, I preached on the topic, "What Can We Say About Abortion?" My outline was simple: (1) all of life is sacred; (2) a woman's body belongs to that woman – no government, no institution, no man, no other person's conscience has a right to claim the body of a woman; (3) religious zealots are a threat to society's well-being, whether in Afghanistan, Northern Ireland or Florida; and (4) we can respect the rights of others and enter into genuine dialogue with those with whom we disagree if they permit it. The sermon was well received and widely distributed. The Sunday following Easter, usually a "low" Sunday, proved to be something of a central Florida "high."

I have already referred to ecumenicity as a fundamental expression of my ministry (Chapter IV). When I first arrived in Winter Park I sought out Walter Horlander. We had worked together in Indiana where he was a member of the state Council of Churches staff. He had become Executive Director of the Florida Council of Churches and was a member of my Winter Park congregation. I soon found myself on the Board of Directors of the Florida Council representing the United Church of Christ. I served as its President in 1995 and 1996. When Horlander retired I chaired the search committee that brought Fred Morris, a former missionary to Brazil and a gifted journalist and teacher, to be his successor. I was also a co-founder of the Interfaith Alliance of Central Florida and fully intend to continue my ecumenical and interfaith activities until the day I die.

On September 19, just eight days after the catastrophic leveling of the Twin Towers in lower Manhattan and the attack on the Pentagon, an interfaith Prayer Service for Peace and Unity was held in the large auditorium of one of Orlando's major hotels. A standing-room-only crowd gathered to hear readings from the Hebrew Bible, the New Testament and the

Koran. There were prayers in Arabic, Hebrew and English. The head of the Husseini Islamic Center spoke, as did a rabbi, a Sikh, a Hindu, the director of the Florida Council of Churches and myself. As always, but even more so now, there is no place in our nation and world for tribal self-consciousness, religious arrogance and sectarian turf-protection. We are – each one of us – called to be "agents of reconciliation" and servants of righteous peace.

I preached my final sermon from the pulpit of Winter Park's First Congregational Church on Easter, April 4, 1999. It was a marvelous day! My son John and his wife had driven down from Georgia to be with us. Other family members would show up a week later for my retirement bash. Preaching on, "The Omega and the Alpha," I said:

> A resurrection faith speaks of more than survival beyond a Holocaust, more than cities and nations rising out of the ashes of violent harm, even more than personal immortality, more than life after death. If the resurrection provides us with a life-principle it speaks of fresh starts and new beginnings, here and now, for each and all of us.

My life at Broward Community College in southern Florida had been a fresh start, as was my life with Pagán International and the Center for Dialogue and Development, as was my teaching at Iliff, and, as most certainly, was my ministry in Winter Park. On a more personal level, my life with Sue, Allison and Eve had been a new beginning. As my ministry at First Church was drawing to a close so too was my life with Sue. In my farewell sermon I said, "Beyond the traumatic bump in the road – whatever it may be – there is hope." Paul said it: "In hope we are saved." *(Romans 8:24)* How richly blest had been my life since that bleak day in 1983. Nor was Easter, 1999, the end of the road. There were still more acts to follow.

SHARON

Sharon Owen, a long-time active member of First Church, came to mean more and more to me as the weeks and months passed. She had married young and had completed her undergraduate studies in New York City while working and mothering three little ones. Returning to Florida (she had done much of her growing up in Florida) she continued her homemaking/parenting duties while earning an MBA and serving as chief financial officer for both non-profit and commercial organizations. Divorced for 13 years, she was one of that countless, unheralded number of single mothers who deserve to have a special place reserved for them in the highest reaches of heaven.

Sheri's father had been a career officer in the U.S. Marines. She attended 12 public schools, from Hawaii to southern California to Florida, in 12 years. Like many military "brats" she had few roots and struggled for a sense of personal identity. With intelligence, perseverance and fierce determination, she grew. With a failed marriage behind her she waited for her youngest daughter, Heather, to graduate from high school before permitting herself to think of life beyond the nest. But Heather, now a university student, had graduated. Suzy, also a student, was on her own and bound for the altar. And her oldest, Chris, was married and moving ahead with his life.

So Sheri developed a "laundry list" of traits she would look for in a potential partner. He would have to be "gentle," "kind," "loving," "understanding," "worldly," both "passionate" and "compassionate," "liberal," "freethinking" and "broad-minded," "intelligent," "a good listener and communicator" with "the wisdom of Solomon and the patience of Job." Hah! No such creature exists. But, that's what she dared hope for.

Today we have a cup sitting atop our refrigerator. It bears an inscription:

> WANTED
> a man
> secure enough
> to do laundry,
> wash dishes,
> run the sweeper,
> dust, cook,
> clean the bathroom –
> and strong enough to
> fool around afterward!

She has inked a strong black line through WANTED and has substituted FOUND.

I had a laundry list too. I was aging, certainly no bargain at any price. I needed someone who would understand what she was getting into (whoever really does?), someone who would admire as well as love me, who would identify with my causes and ideals, share my values and somewhat agnostic belief-system, someone with a keen sense of humor who would offer emotional strength, physical compatibility and intellectual stimulus. (Although a "bean-counter," Sharon's extra-curricular interests embrace astronomy, politics, archeology, cooking, movies, and old *I Love Lucy* reruns.)

On April 8, 2000, we were married in an ornate little 19th century chapel. Douglas Fitch, now senior minister of Glide Memorial Church in San Francisco, a friend and colleague of many years, flew across the continent to officiate. Sheri and I had attended Glide in the late summer of '99. Doug had preached. As we left the packed church she said, "If we ever get married I want him to do it." He did.

The service was moving in its simplicity with only family and close friends in attendance. Sharon's three youngsters "gave her away" (that archaic phrase was not used). My son, John, was my best man. He offered a toast to his old man at the reception that brought tears to my eyes. It compared favorably to those loquacious toasts offered by Hugh Grant in the film, "Four Weddings and a Funeral." Leslye and her little family were there, as was dear Allison who had crossed the country to represent her side of the family. To me the service was almost perfect. Sharon was by my side as were children from earlier marriages. Those marriages, imperfect as they may have been, offered us seasons of genuine meaning and fulfillment, and gave us our children, now adults, who will carry our roots and dreams into the future.

In these pages I have written of my life with my first wife, Phyllis, as well as describing life shared with Sue, and now Sheri. Why so much personal material? Because, when I resigned as a UMC bishop, I said, "I would have friend and foe alike draw hard lessons from my example..." Our lives dare not be compartmentalized. While functioning as a student, a pastor, a bishop, a corporate executive and teacher, I have also been a husband and father, for better and worse. I have confessed faults and frailties, painfully acknowledging my feet of clay. But, life is growth, and I pray that with the passage of time I have gained new insights, learned to assume more responsibilities and deepened my commitments to loved ones. Those of us who claim to serve the Nazarene are called to put first things first, and nothing takes precedence over covenantal relationships. Why review one's life-journey unless the story can prove helpful to others? I pray this will do that.

My ministry continues. I teach corporate ethics at Rollins College and courses on preaching, pastoral identity, ministerial ethics, pastoral psychology and servant ministries at the South Florida Center for Theological Studies. I lead workshops and retreats, consult with local churches, continue a limited counseling ministry and have resumed some long-neglected writing. However – and this is a grace-filled plus – I can say "no" when I choose, opt out of pointless meetings, and invest time and energy in my family. If this be retirement I recommend it highly!

On August 15, 1999, after a six-month search, the First Congregational Church called Bryan Fulwider to be its Senior Minister. Bryan, a distinguished young clergyman from Little Rock, is a former student of mine. In 1985, he was the first recipient of the Ronald E. Sleeth Award for Outstanding Preacher of the Year at Iliff. A fine preacher, a sensitive and faithful pastor and a skilled administrator, with impressive ecumenical credentials as President of the Arkansas Interfaith Alliance and Chair of his denomination's Conference Commission on Christian Unity and Interreligious Concerns, he is leading "my" beloved congregation into a bold and wondrous future.

※

At the time of my resignation from the episcopacy a noted cartoonist sent me one of his Friar Tuck cartoons. The chubby friar was in the foreground with hands clasped and a tear running down his cheek. The cross and empty tomb were faintly outlined in the background. The caption? "Bishop Armstrong: While I'm resigned to your resignation I also rejoice in the promise of the resurrection!" It is another treasured item that hangs on my workroom wall.

In December, 1983, Spurgeon Dunnam, editor of the *United Methodist Reporter*, wrote of my "tragic fall from the pinnacle of success." His comments were both pastoral and penetrating. He concluded his editorial by saying:

> I do not know when or under what circumstances, but I will be very surprised and disappointed if James Armstrong has made his last positive contribution to God's kingdom.(2)

Spurgeon is no longer with us, but I hope this account brings some measure of gratification to him as he "looks down" upon us from wherever he may be.

EPILOGUE AS PROLOGUE

Faith may be a leap for some; more important, it is a process. If we are becoming what we one day will be it follows that the faith we live by develops with us – or we develop with it. Fifty years ago my faith was an exciting discovery. A decision had been made and a risk had been taken. Today my faith runs much deeper and is far broader. It has been forged on an anvil of good fortune and misfortune. Influenced by human frailty and exposed to harsh reality, shaped by bitter loss and disappointment as well as peaks of joy and satisfaction, it has evolved. It has sustained me, providing meaning, direction, motivation and a sense of reassuring security.

There is no discounting the religious atmosphere of my childhood home. In that setting it seems natural that at the age of 16 I "accepted Christ as my Savior" although I wasn't sure what that meant, and the rush and blush of the trip to the altar passed quickly. However, my return to the church when I was 20, my response to the call to ministry, and the rapid succession of decisions made on the basis of what amounted to genuine conversion experience (my course was radically changed), launched me and my young family on an irreversible journey.

At first Jesus Christ was at the heart of my quest. My faith was Christocentric. No more. I have changed. As a believer I still claim Jesus of Nazareth as my Lord. His love ethic guides my understanding of the Bible and, I hope, my daily walk. His cross and resurrection define the roles of other-centered service and sacrifice and the ultimate triumph of Spirit in human experience. But, if the Nazarene carpenter and teacher pointed beyond himself to God should I not do the same?

It was G.A. Studdert-Kennedy writing from the trenches of France during the First World War who said, "It is God alone that matters."(1) That "God" is a far more awesome and profound concept and reality than the "born-again" bumper-sticker zealots with their "Jesus only" witness seem to understand. "Jesus saves" may be a meaningful slogan to some but it doesn't begin to exhaust the truth of God's self-revelations.

One can gaze at Michelangelo's God in the Sistine Chapel, a massive, bearded, all-powerful, anthropomorphic God, and miss the point entirely. God is not a super-macho Moses any more than God is a jazzed-up feminine Grandma Moses. *God is God!* First Cause, Ground of Being, Ultimate Reality, Creator, Sustainer – all of these and more. Call God by whatever name, the *reality* cannot be reduced to our size, defined by our terms, or limited to our understanding.

God is not American, not European, not African, not Asian; God is neither black nor white, male nor female. God is not a Buddhist or Hindu or Muslim or Jew. Hard as it may be for some of us to accept, God is not a Christian. God is not earthbound. God is ever beyond our xenophobic, ethnic and religious categories. As we move into the 21st century our theology must come to terms with global and cosmic reality.

It was believed that the earth was the center of the universe until the Polish astronomer, Copernicus, insisted that the sun and not the earth is the center of our universe. The British philosopher, John Hick, has called for a Copernican revolution in religious thought. A pre-Copernican notion argues that one's own religion is the center of the religious universe and the touchstone for all other religious points of view. The post-Copernican view insists that no religious system has a right to assert that it is one with the truth of God or the will of God in any final sense. No belief-system should presume to say that its creeds explain the fullness of divine truth.(2)

Our world view has expanded since the time of Copernicus. From Kepler and Galileo through Albert Einstein and Stephen Hawking, we have been on a thrilling journey through time and space. New stars are being discovered every day and we are told that trillions of heavenly bodies orbit through their respective universes. Does this mean that the concept of God no longer serves a useful purpose? Certainly not. Even the most advanced thinkers of our time leave room for Mystery and Spirit, for an Ultimate Reality, for a Parent Truth that makes all lesser truth cohesive.

What does all of this mean to me as a Christian? Christians believe that God is not only a Creator and Sustainer, but a Parent God. "When you pray say, 'Our Father...'." God, we say, is a *personal* God. We say that we believe that Jesus was God's unique son. And, we believe in the Holy Spirit, the breath of life that infuses all personal existence. We say, many of us, that we are "trinitarian." But again, it is unthinkable to limit God to three and only three manifestations, or to philosophical theories originating in the 4th and 5th centuries.

Just as modern science has enabled our world views to expand and mature, so too has our increasing awareness of other peoples, cultures and belief-systems, enabled us to enlarge the vistas of our faith. Retired Bishop John Shelby Spong, that refreshing, far-out, counter voice of the Episcopal Church, has written, "Most Christians are woefully ignorant of the truth and beauty of other religions...(and) our ignorance breeds prejudice."(3) Valued tradition and our own experience tell us that God is personal. We are not alone in that view. True, Paul Tillich's Ground of Being can be understood in non-personal ways, and Tillich was a Christian. But, Spong reminds us that "that range of understanding between the personal...and the non-personal...can, in fact, be found in most religious traditions...Hinduism, Buddhism, Islam, Judaism...(as well as) Christianity, have within them wide varieties and highly developed separate schools of thought"(4) that have been influenced as much by cultural, psychological, environmental and political factors as by theological reflection. Ivory-towered academicians who have majored in theological knit-picking, and insulated "believers" who have found refuge in simplistic, irrational religious ideas, may have a hard time dealing with this expanding, exploding approach to revelation, but it, in fact, represents informed, enlightened thought as well as common sense. Under an inclusive umbrella it makes ample room for Mohandas Gandhi the Hindu, Rabbi Abraham Heschel, Thich Nhat Hanh the Buddhist, and "all sorts and conditions" of faithful people. *No one of us, no group, no tribe, has a lock on God's truth.*

As I think of God two words, "Mystery" and "Spirit," inform my understanding. I am no longer Christocentric. Mystery is that which is ever beyond our grasp, but Mystery provides a framework for a believable theocentricity. Spirit is God with and in us; God omnipresent. The Hebrew word for "breath" doesn't quite do it, nor does the Pentecostal fire of Peter, nor the powerful, moving poetry of Paul, unless we broaden the net to make it universal. "The Spirit itself testifies with our spirits that we are God's children, and if children heirs also, heirs of God and fellow heirs with Christ, if we really share his suffering in order to share his glory too." *(Romans 8:16,17)*

Our belief in the God of the universes, an informed appreciation of the legitimacy of other religions, and a firm conviction that Spirit is at work among and within all peoples of the earth, is directly related to our understanding the role the church is called upon to play in the 21st century.

The church is in the process of reinventing and rebuilding itself, and the emerging church, as Loren Mead and others have pointed out, will recognize the central importance of the local congregation as "a community of common values...shaped by a story within a larger, hostile environment."(5) The love ethic of Jesus, a commitment to the gospel of the cross and resurrection, joined by a passionate embrace and celebration of the diversity in our own communities and around the world, and a new global consciousness, sharply at odds with a self-serving, parochial, materialistic, hedonistic culture, will hopefully shape the Christian presence and witness in the world of tomorrow.

I continue to be committed to the church I have sought to serve and the interfaith movement to which I have given myself. But, both denominational and ecumenical agencies are changing before our very eyes. Denominational self-consciousness, hierarchical posturing and prerogatives, sinful ecclesiastical competition, self-serving goals and small-mindedness must give way to a new reality – a truly inclusive church that is not preoccupied with self-preservation and empire building, but that is a prophetic servant fellowship, a shepherd church, offering itself to a confused and battered world beyond its boundaries.

❦

I have called this epilogue "prologue" because it ends with new beginnings. I have tried to spell out some of the life-forces, sympathies, and convictions that have given direction to both my personal and professional journeys. Beyond that initial leap many years ago my faith has been in process, nor is my journey yet complete. My faith is not a finished product. As its dimensions have evolved, however, it has brought me to this point and I am grateful.

It has been a great life, but, as I have confessed, it has been marred and tainted. Harry Emerson Fosdick concluded his classic sermon on, "The Forgiveness of Sins," with the word: "For your soul's sake get rid of (your sin). But there is only one way. Whatever theology you hold, it is the way of the cross – penitence, confession, restitution, pardon."(6) I know those steps by heart. Believe me, in spite of the wonderful gifts that life has showered upon me, I have been and continue to be "heartily sorry for these my misdoings." I close each day with a silent prayer for those my actions have harmed. But, forgiveness has been granted, grace has been claimed, the promise of my personal world was restored, and ministry, refocused and renewed, has continued. The novelist was wrong. There *are* second acts in our lives, and sometimes third, fourth and fifth acts. My cartoonist friend was right. I *do* "rejoice…in the promise of the resurrection."

JUNE OF 2000

There is a pause of Time,
Many moments crowd our minds
As we think back with fondness,
And forward with faith.
Change comes, at once slowly and quickly,
And as the clock ticks,
We find ourselves in the present!
And the future is now!
Memory moves us forward through the past,
When we win the race of life,
And our endings are our beginnings.(1)

–Arthur Charles Finmann

NOTES

Introduction

1. F. Scott Fitzgerald, *The Great Gatsby*.
2. *St. Petersburg Times,* August 12, 1984.

II. "If I Had A Thousand Lives To Live"

1. Stefan Zweig, *Three Masters,* pp. 124, 125.
2. Nicolai Berdyaev, *Dostoevsky,* p. 57.
3. Bellah and others, *Habits of the Heart,* p. 47.
4. Paul Johnson, *Personality and Religion,* Abingdon, 1957, chapter 2.
5. Kirschenbaum, *On Being Carl Rogers,* Delta, 1979, p. 394.
6. Alfred T. Davies, editor, *The Pulpit Speaks On Race,* Abingdon, 1968, chapter 1.
7. Karen Lebacqz and Joseph D. Driskill, *Ethics and Spiritual Care,* Abingdon, 2000.
8. Karen Lebacqz and Ronald G. Barton, *Sex in the Parish,* John Knox/Westminster, 1991.
9. H. Newton Maloney, et. al., *Clergy Malpractice,* Westminster Press, 1986.
10. Robert Gildea, "The Church That Refuses to Die," *Together,* October, 1967.
11. Thomas J. Mullen, *The Dialogue Gap,* Abingdon, 1969, p. 114.
12. Rudiger Reitz, *The Church in Experiment,* Abingdon, 1969, p. 68.

III. "You Ain't Fit To Be No Methodist Preacher"

1. Fremont Powers, *Indianapolis News,* July 31, 1968.
2. Paul Moore, *Presences: A Bishop's Life in the City,* Farrar, Straus and Giraux, 1997, pp. 156, 157.
3. Paul Moore Jr., *Take A Bishop Like Me,* Harper and Row, 1979, p. 110.
4. Ibid., p. 24.
5. Charles C. Manz, *The Leadership Wisdom of Jesus,* Barrett-Koehler Publishers, 1998.
6. Stanlev Bing, *Crazy Bosses: Spotting Them, Serving Them, Surviving Them.*
7. James MacGregor Burns, *Leadership,* Harper and Row, 1978, p. 20.
8. Joanne B. Ciulila, editor, *Ethics: the Heart of Leadership,* Praeger, 1998, p. xii.
9. M. Scott Peck, *The Different Drum,* Touchstone, 1987, p. 63.
10. Robert K. Greenleaf, *Servant Leadership: A Journey Into the Nature of Legitimate Power and Greatness,* Paulist Press, 1977.
11. G. Lloyd Rediger, *Clergy Killers,* Westminster/John Knox, 1997.
12. Roy Howard Beck, *United Methodist Reporter.*

IV. "A Leader Must Be A Bridge"

1. Raymond Bosier, *The Criterion.*
2. "Flickering Candles at NCC Birthday Fest," *The Christian Century,* November 18, 1981, p. 1189.
3. *Indianapolis Star,* November 8, 1981.
4. James M. Wall, "The Buckley Line: Firing From the Right," *The Christian Century,* November 3, 1982, p. 1091f.
5. A. James Rudin, *Israel for Christians: Understanding Modern Israel,* Fortress Press, 1983, p. 140.

6. James M. Wall, "Worship Powers WCC Assembly," *The Christian Century*, August 17-24, 1983, p. 732.
7. "Activism and Reconciliation Were Themes of Bishop Armstrong," *Michigan Christian Advocate*, November 28, 1983.

V. "I Am Absolutely Responsible"

1. see: Merle Miller, *Plain Speaking*, Berkley Books, 1984, p. 422.
2. see: Gary L. Harbaugh, *Pastor As Person*, Augsburg, 1984, chapter 1.
3. Russell Chandler, *RNA Newsletter*, December, 1983.
4. *Playboy*, September, 1986, p. 54.

VI. "The Call Has Not Been Canceled"

1. Elaine Louie, "After Cancer A Whole New Attitude," *New York Times*.
2. Bryan G. Fulwider, "A. James Armstrong: Prophetic Preacher for Today's Social Crisis," *An Intellectual History of Iliff*, 1999, p. 416.

VII. "New Alphas"

1. *The Carillon*, April, 1999.
2. Spurgeon Dunnam III, "Reflections on a Bishop's Tragic Fall from the Pinnacle of Success," *United Methodist Reporter*, December 2, 1983.

Epilogue As Prologue

1. G.A. Studdert-Kennedy, *The Hardest Part*, p. 1.

2. I am indebted to John Shelby Spong's *Into the Whirlwind: the Future of the Church*, chapter 13, for his insights into the Ptolemic, Copernican and post-Copernican stages of religious development.
3. John Shelby Spong, *Into the Whirlwind,* Seabury, 1983, p. 182.
4. Ibid., p. 182.
5. Loren Mead, *The Once and Future Church,* The Alban Institute, 1991.
6. Harry Emerson Fosdick, *Riverside Sermons,* Harper, 1958, p. 292f.

June of 2000

1. *United Church News,* June 2000, p. 3.

ABOUT THE AUTHOR

James Armstrong was born in 1924. Married just out of high school, he went to college, seminary, and pursued graduate studies while serving Methodist churches. Following a ten-year stint at a huge Midwestern church, he was elected to the episcopacy in 1968, the youngest United Methodist bishop in the U.S. A distinguished preacher, he was called "the most activist bishop" in the nation. He served as President of the National Council of Churches and was deeply involved in the civil rights movement, the peace movement, and a variety of controversial causes. After acknowledging that he had been unfaithful to his wife, he resigned from the episcopacy in 1983 and disappeared from the public eye, only to resurface as a seminary professor, a local church pastor, and an ecumenical officer. Now retired, he teaches at Rollins College and the South Florida Center for Theological Studies. This is his story, but, as he indicates, it is not finished yet.

ABOUT GREATUNPUBLISHED.COM

www.greatunpublished.com is a website that exists to serve writers and readers, and to remove some of the commercial barriers between them. When you purchase a GreatUNpublished title, whether you order it in electronic form or in a paperback volume, the author is receiving a majority of the post-production revenue.

A GreatUNpublished book is never out of stock, and always available, because each book is printed on-demand, as it is ordered.

A portion of the site's share of profits is channeled into literacy programs.

So by purchasing this title from GreatUNpublished, you are helping to revolutionize the publishing industry for the benefit of writers and readers.

And for this we thank you.